POVERTY

IN THE

UNITED STATES

WHY IT'S A BLIGHT ON THE AMERICAN PSYCHE

— HOW WE CAN WIPE IT OUT —

ROBERT S. PFEIFFER

ISBN: 978-1-54395-134-9 (print)
ISBN: 978-1-54395-135-6 (ebook)

FOREWORD

"Overcoming poverty is not a gesture of charity. It is an act of justice. It is the protection of a fundamental human right, the right to dignity and a decent life."

— *Nelson Mandela, former President of South Africa*

I'm often asked why I got involved in the war on poverty. I grew up in the middle class and never experienced hunger or a lack of possessions. Like millions of Americans, I suffered my share of hard times when I struggled to make ends meet. There is nothing unusual about that.

But I've experienced things that made a lasting impression on me, such as knowing the Mexican-American foreman who taught me the construction trade and worked incredibly hard, but couldn't afford to buy toys for his children. Or watching a roommate in Vail, Colorado, spend the winter skiing on unemployment benefits when there were plenty of jobs available. I've watched many of my friends struggle financially. I was lucky, however, because I never experienced poverty.

It wasn't personal experiences that fired my interest in poverty. Instead it was a desire, a need to give back to those less fortunate than I. Throughout my career I volunteered at organizations that aided the poor and tried to help out financially. I was on the board of a nonprofit foundation that parceled money to charities that helped impoverished people in my community. I went on mission trips to help the poor, volunteered at homeless shelters and food banks, and supported similar causes.

But I can't say that my experiences with the poor were very different from those of other Americans who felt the same way.

The important question is not why I got involved with organizations that sought to help the poor. I knew many people who did what they could. A more important question is why I felt compelled to write a book on the subject. The answer is simple. It's because I "worked the problem," for want of a better phrase.

For many years I worked for a CEO who would hand me a complex situation and ask me to "work the problem." I always had a knack for that and loved doing it. I'm a CPA and self-confessed data nerd. Complex problems — which I love to tackle — are opportunities to research, analyze, simplify and conclude. I went through this process with poverty in the United States because I wanted to understand it and get past any stereotypes I had because they clouded my understanding of the subject. I didn't know how to reconcile social justice, "welfare mooching," hungry children, biblical values, enabling dependency, single moms and addiction. What should govern my thoughts and how should I approach this multi-tentacle enigma?

I devoted seven years to researching the subject. I read anything I could find on it, which included scholarly books and countless articles and research papers. I traveled a great deal, which gave me the opportunity to interview many people. I worked with the poor in lots of different capacities. When I finished I wanted to share what I learned with other Americans.

I was not alone in my confusion. An obvious given is that poverty is a blight on the American psyche. That is because a nation as wealthy as ours should not have so many people living in poverty. In our hearts and souls, we know that we can help and should help. The troubling question is this: "Is our time and money really making a difference?" Complicating this issue is a massive labyrinth of complex government programs we barely understand. Should we throw our hands in the air and rely on them to solve the problem? We've learned that that approach is a cop-out, because the government has barely made a dent at solving the poverty issue. On a macro scale, it is poorly understood and politically divisive. In sum, unlike many social issues, there is little consensus about how we should manage it.

The good news is that my research cleared my thinking on poverty and pointed me in the right direction. I figured out how the government is approaching the issue, and, more important, I learned how I should spend my time and resources. I learned the difference between comfortable and effective compassion. I was convinced that with the right approach, we, the American people, could have a meaningful impact on poverty. And I strongly believed I could help others focus their thoughts and actions with more confidence and success. I knew I could help us be better warriors in the war on poverty. That is my hope and prayer.

Robert S. Pfeiffer

TABLE OF CONTENTS

I

VOLUNTEERISM

Shoe drive in Sterling, Colorado, with some of the volunteers and kids

I handed him the box of tennis shoes, and he clutched it to his body in stubborn desperation. He was just four years old, shy and quiet. But now that he had those shoes, his assertiveness surfaced. He was holding on for dear life. "Oh no," I thought. "I'm supposed to leave the box with the cashier, but that means my little friend is going to have to let go of it."

We were in the midst of a shoe drive, giving free shoes to all the kids in a Head Start preschool in Sterling, Colorado. The procedures were to let the kids pick out shoes, then we were to box them, write the recipient's name on the box and take them to the cashier.

I tried to explain all that to the four-year-old face looking up at me, but he wasn't buying it. His eyes were intense, the gaze questioning. His excitement in picking out the shoes had moved to fear of losing them. He didn't trust me to ever give them back.

It seemed we needed to make an exception to the procedures as it related to my little friend.

So we went to the cashier together, and I lifted him up, and the clerk scanned the label within his clutching hands. He never let go. Not from the time he sat down with the rest of his class to the time they got back on the bus and went back to preschool. God bless him.

It's the innocent ones that tug at our hearts the hardest. I smiled as I saw the little boy climb the big stairs of the bus holding his new shoes for dear life. I made a difference in his life that day, but it felt very small. I wondered about his family, his education, the influences around him. I wondered where those little shoes would walk, and as he grows up, where the larger sizes would take him.

As we were organizing the shoe drive, I was concerned we would be taken advantage of by the kids or their families. But as I handed out shoes, my worry shifted to another concern: I wanted to do more. I felt petty — one pair of $18 shoes to fight against all the odds that small child faces.

I'm not alone. Americans all over the country share these same feelings. We are a giving and charitable people. We want to help the poor and those less fortunate than us.

According to Gallup, 83% of us donate to charity, and 65% of us volunteer our time.[1] But is it enough? I asked myself, How many people were like me — happy to help but wondering how much of a difference they really made?

As a society we are good at giving things away — shoes, food, even housing. But the human being on the other end is what matters most, and it's the rare charity that teaches life skills and prepares the poor to reach for the American Dream. Nor is our federal government any good at that; its role is to formulize benefits and hand them out.

There is great truth in the Chinese proverb: "Give a man a fish, and you feed him for a day; teach a man to fish, and you feed him for a lifetime." That's a bigger issue we're barely dealing with. That is what I was feeling watching my little friend climb the steps on the bus. His new shoes will take him only so far.

2

POVERTY: THE GREAT DIVIDER

Rarely do we find men who willingly engage in hard, solid thinking. There is an almost universal quest for easy answers and half-baked solutions. Nothing pains some people more than having to think.

— *Dr. Martin Luther King Jr.* [2]

Shaleec Thomas and Debbie Stone, volunteers at Care Placement Services

"Get rid of the poverty pimps," is how Shaleec Thomas answered my question as to what she thought would be the most important thing we could do to eliminate poverty.[3] Shaleec is a young black women living in public housing, volunteering her time at various nonprofit causes. She explained that poverty pimps were people, government programs and charities that prey on the poor and profit from them as well.

Thomas's answer surprised me, but then again about half of what I read and experience in the world of poverty surprises me. When I asked Debbie Stone, formerly a homeless mother working in a nonprofit employment agency, the same question, she said she would get rid of "cliffs." [4] It meant that people can lose more in government benefits than they make when they find a job. I thought that was a term used by policy wonks, but it is used on the streets. That surprised me, too.

I was getting used to being surprised. For example, learning that Ronald Reagan started the largest welfare program we have today, the EITC (Earned Income Tax Credit), which supports low-wage workers with kids. Or finding out that Franklin Delano Roosevelt believed handouts were counter-productive, saying, "The Federal Government must and shall quit this business of relief." [5] I'm surprised that Bill Clinton said his mother "still got up every day, no matter what the hell was going on, and she got herself ready and went to work.... It kept food on the table, but it gave us a sense of pride and meaning and direction.... I couldn't imagine what it would be like for a child to grow up in a home where the child never saw anybody go to work...." [6] I'm also surprised Mother Teresa said: "We have no right to judge the rich. For our part, what we desire is not a class struggle but a class encounter, in which the rich save the poor and the poor save the rich." [7]

I always assumed poverty was complex and that I had much to learn, but now I know that was an understatement. My years of volunteering, studying and interviewing those in and around poverty have proved that to me. I have also learned that perhaps no issue in the U.S. is as controversial as poverty and welfare. They are issues with a storied past fought about on political battle lines decades old. Even indisputable facts are often in heated dispute. We hear news reports describing a growing problem about the downtrodden, such as half of our kids are going hungry or that homelessness is running rampant. But I also hear that many in poverty own their own homes or stories about welfare cheats boasting about their free cellphones.

Sadly, Americans have a shallow understanding of poverty and absolutely no consensus as to how to fight it. How did things get so confused and politicized?

President Johnson signs the Food Stamp Act in 1964

It didn't happen overnight. We have been confusing and deluding ourselves for about six decades. In the 1960s Lyndon Johnson established his Great Society programs and declared a "war on poverty." [8] We created programs, spent lots of money and fought for more than 20 years to eradicate poverty. But by 1988 President Reagan avowed, "We declared a war on poverty and poverty won." [9] Even so we fought on, increasing spending and creating programs. Eight years later, in 1996, President Clinton passed welfare reform in order to fix the system. Since then we have spent 22 years expanding and tweaking programs, forming and giving to charities and volunteering our time. When we look at the numbers, 12.3% of the population is in poverty, pretty much where it was in 1966. As proof, about half the American population cite the fact that we have failed. The other half cite this fact as evidence that we're not doing enough.

Perhaps I can shed some light on all of this by asking, "Where are we, and what should we do?" We all agree that we want fewer people in poverty and that we have resources to deal with the problem.

I'm just a citizen, a married father of five, a CPA, a businessman and smack in the middle class. After 30 years of study, working with the poor, evaluating foundations and charities, wading through our welfare programs, studying experts' reports and reading their books, I'm happy to share what I know. I also created a website called FederalSafetyNet.com to pass along my knowledge. The site climbed to the top three sites on a Google search of U.S. welfare programs.

Here is what I learned: I believe it is citizens like you and me who have to solve this problem. The experts rarely address the whole picture — government, charity and individual citizen efforts. They are often on the wrong track. For example, studying the nutritional value of school lunches. Or they might have an agenda and spend their time and energy advancing it. I have none. I'm just a guy trying to sort out a problem I strongly believe to be solvable. I see my job as taking all that data, summarizing it and simplifying it so we can take the view from the top of the hill, see where we are and make improvements. After all, we know the poor well because we live with them, work with them, are relatives to them. In short, we've been them and we are them. We need to take a critical look and use our skills, knowledge and wisdom to dramatically improve the poverty stats. I'm convinced we can do it with a little thought and analysis and a whole lot of common sense. I'll walk you through my thought process and propose some postulates to build on. I'd be surprised if you don't agree.

There is nothing revolutionary in this book as to how to address our problems. Quite the contrary. We have allowed simple facts to be sidetracked by thousands of charities, complex government programs and a belief we can sit back and let the experts handle things. Enough. We have to get involved and when we do, good things will happen.

The poor

Let's start with defining the poor. There are all kinds of poor people — old and young, minorities and white, sick and healthy, once prosperous and never prosperous. Some of the poor are happy because they require little to be content, others are anxious about their situation and still others are bitter. "Poor" as used in this book simply means having little money. It isn't a comment about education, history, attitude or motivation. Defining the word poor is often muddied because it has two definitions. The first is "having little money or few possessions." The second is "worse than usual, expected or inferior quality." I use the first definition. I assume everyone has immeasurable worth.

If we expand the definition of poor, it also means "not having enough money for the basic things people need to live properly." This definition arouses our compassion. It is the basis for our welfare programs and our charities.

Now the simplest categorization of the poor: I've put them in two categories. The first is those who cannot help themselves and the second is those who can help themselves. The mentally and physically disabled are in the first category. They include the mentally impaired and severely disabled veterans. A sophisticated society wants to take care of its citizens in need. The measure of success is pretty straightforward — we want all such people to have comfortable, safe and rewarding lives. We strive to find the resources and care to do that. The second category is trickier. We want to give a "hand up" to this category so that the poor can lead lives of financial independence. How do we do that? It takes much more thought — and is the focus of this book.

It is difficult in America today to have a meaningful discussion about the poor and to address the effectiveness of charities or welfare. We have lost our ability to communicate and analyze. We talk past each other constantly.

The first problem is that we don't establish who it is we are talking about. Is it the innocent hungry child or the homeless woman on the street? Is it the single black mother or the 20-year-old community college student? Is it the welfare cheat or the chronic alcoholic living on the streets? Is it the starving senior or the surfer on food stamps? It makes a huge difference. Giving money to an alcoholic isn't the same as giving money to a single mother. Distributing a free school lunch to a middle-class child is different from giving one to a child from a poor neighborhood. Who is it we are talking about? We are turning into the Zax — the Dr. Seuss creatures that stare and holler at each other and never budge. [10]

This is an accurate depiction as to how we treat issues of the poor and welfare reform today. The polarizing forces on the left and right have us stymied. One side says people need help, and that is proof enough to spend more. The other side says government is causing the problem, so cut back and do less. When we argue at that level, nothing gets resolved. We must get into the details. We must address who we are talking about, what we are trying to do, the makeup of our programs and charities, whom they serve and their effectiveness. We can't just be progressive or conservative for big or small government, for more redistribution or against more dependency. Let's look at the various people in poverty and do some critical thinking. It will require an open heart, honest analysis and tough decisions. It is easier to sit back and blame the other side for all the problems, but that won't help the poor or the plight of the poor.

The first thing we need to do is figure out who we are talking about. Let's start with poverty. What is it? What part of the population compose it?

A marvelous woman, Mollie Orshansky, nicknamed Ms. Poverty by her colleagues and friends, can help us. Read on.

3

WHO ARE WE TALKING ABOUT?

If it is not possible to state unequivocally "how much is enough," it should be possible to assert with confidence how much, on an average, is too little.

— *Mollie Orshansky* [11]

Mollie Orshansky of the Social Security Administration

You have to hand it to Mollie Orshansky of the Social Security Administration. For over 50 years, her definition of poverty has held up. In 1963 she established a definition of poverty as she worked on a research project about poverty and children. At that time there was no standard to measure poverty, so she created one. She started with the cost of a minimum food diet, according to the Department of Agriculture. She figured that if you can't feed yourself adequately, then you are in poverty. She further postulated that food should be only one-third of a household budget, because that was the average experience of families at the time. Then voila! A poverty threshold surfaced. Below that income level, a person or family was "in poverty" and above it was not.

Orshansky grew up poor and was the first in her family to go to college, where she got a degree in mathematics and statistics. She once said, "If I write about the poor, I don't need a good imagination — I have a good memory." She worked as an economist and statistician for 40 years for the federal government and died at the age of 91.

U.S. Poverty Threshold

	Annual Income
One person household	$12,488
Two person household	$15,877
Three person household	$19,515
Four person household	$25,094
Five person household	$29,714
Six person household	$33,618

Orshansky never intended for her simple calculation to be used as the definition of poverty in America for 50 years, but that is exactly what happened. And why not? It is very useful to have an income cutoff that defines poverty and lets us see how many people are below that number. That is why Orshansky's method has lasted so long. Her calculation of poverty has been increased by the cost of living over the past 50 years, but otherwise her numbers are the foundation for defining poverty to this day. The accompanying table shows the poverty threshold for the year 2017.[12]

Based on the poverty threshold, we have a good handle on poverty in America. More precisely, we have a good handle on who makes what income in America. We know the spread, because the Census Bureau tracks income from all households in America so that income means wages from jobs, self-employment or investments. Based on the spread of income in the U.S., 12.3% of the U.S. population has income below the threshold and are "in poverty." That equates to 39.7 million people, 12.8 million of them children.

The first poverty controversy hits us right away: Is Orshansky's definition right? Can a single person actually live on an income of $12,488 for a year? Or can a family of four live on $25,094 a year? How far off do you think the number is? If you think the number should be 1.5 times the poverty threshold, then 21.0% of the population, or 67.6 million people, are in poverty. If you think it should be twice the threshold, then 29.7% of the population is in poverty. Half the threshold would mean 5.7% of the population is in poverty.[13]

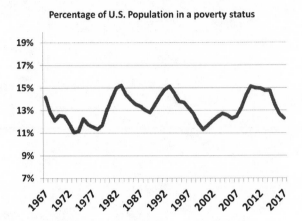

Percentage of U.S. Population in a poverty status

Using the poverty threshold applicable to that year,[14] the chart to the left shows the percentage of the population in poverty over the past 50 years. For 50 years, the percentage of the population in poverty has hovered around 12%–15%. In good times or bad, we seem to have about one in seven people in the U.S. in poverty. Some people move through poverty quickly when they are young or hard times hit them, but far too many reside in a poverty status for years. If we look at the most recent Census data report on poverty mobility, 58% of those in poverty in 2009 were still in poverty four years later, at the start of 2013.[15]

No matter how you slice it, we have too many people in poverty in our nation. We can all look subjectively at Orshansky's poverty threshold number and know it is pretty tough to live on that little income. We can agree that we have too many people trying to do just that. This isn't a reflection as to how they live after charity or welfare. It is not a conclusion on their motivation, skills or history. It is a simple fact that we have about 40 million Americans who are not living financially independent of charities and welfare. For whatever reason, history or cause, the number is too high, and that takes us to the first postulate of this book:

POSTULATE I

The U.S. has too many people in poverty. To be precise we mean that we have too many people who do not earn enough income on their own to live comfortably and enjoy economic freedom.

We have a problem. We can blame our federal government, but it is not alone in the fight. We also have thousands of charities attacking the problem, from food banks to homeless shelters. We have big foundations with smart people allocating millions to the battle. Still the number of people in poverty remains stubbornly high in good or bad times.

If you agree with postulate No. 1, the next question is how do we fix it? Suddenly we are dragged into politics, welfare, charities and history. But before we get there, let's back up and define more precisely what it is we are trying to do. We need to make sure we are clear about the goal. We all know it, but it too often gets lost in the poverty and welfare debate.

4

WHAT ARE WE TRYING TO DO?

We must find ways of returning far more of our dependent people to independence. We must find ways of returning them to a participating and productive role in the community.

— *President John F. Kennedy* [16]

Bob Cote (left) and friend

I met Bob Cote, the guy who had trademarked the saying "a hand up, not a hand out." He headed the organization Step Denver.[17] Cote had been using the saying in the early 1990s as the mission statement of the charity he ran to help alcoholics in Denver. Cote believed the saying depicted the formula for success for charitable organizations.

Cote's formula worked for him and Step Denver, but it may not be appropriate for all charities. If a charity is working with people who are not of sound mind or body and can't help themselves, then a handout is appropriate. I understand Cote's saying as it relates to charities working with people who can help themselves. Cote was working with alcoholics who could change their lives and often did.

Cote's saying is another way of confirming the Chinese proverb quoted in Chapter 1, "Give a man a fish, and you feed him for a day; teach a man to fish, and you feed him for a lifetime." The simple saying is our goal, our mantra.

We want to teach people to fish rather than hand out fish. So as we translate that to the poverty world, we want to help people to be financially independent, not merely to help them endure living in poverty.

POSTULATE
#2

POSTULATE 2

For those with sound mind and body, our goal is to help them achieve economic freedom.

President Kennedy eloquently summed up the problem, "We must find ways of returning far more of our dependent people to independence." That is clearly our goal. But things get tricky when some of us come up short. What do we do then? Should we have welfare or redistribution of income to make up the difference? Is that helpful to our goal? Is it the job of government? Or is it a moral obligation of a strong nation?

Now we have arrived at the political issue at the heart of welfare, charity and compassion. How much welfare or redistribution of income should we have in America? We can turn to two stalwarts on the political right and left for input — Milton Friedman and Dr. Martin Luther King Jr.

5

LIVING WAGE

We might all of us be willing to contribute to the relief of poverty, provided everyone else did. We might not be willing to contribute the same amount without such assurance.... Suppose one accepts, as I do, this line of reasoning as justifying governmental action to alleviate poverty; to set, as it were, a floor under the standard of life of every person in the community.

— *Milton Friedman* [18]

I am now convinced that the simplest approach will prove to be the most effective — the solution to poverty is to abolish it directly by a now widely discussed measure: the guaranteed income.

— *Dr. Martin Luther King Jr.*[19]

Dr. Martin Luther King Jr.   Milton Friedman

Milton Friedman called it the "negative income tax." Dr. Martin Luther King Jr. called it a "guaranteed income." It meant the same to both men — a government payment that would alleviate poverty. Friedman is arguably the most respected conservative economist of the 20th century. And King arguably the most impactful progressive of the 20th century. The two men are far apart on the political spectrum and yet are in agreement on this issue. Both of them argued for a cash program paid by the federal government to alleviate poverty.

The nomenclature today is a "living wage," a standard of income that an individual or family can comfortably live on. As the term implies, it is a wage generated through work.

Our goal is for all to earn a living wage, but what happens if they don't or can't? That is where both Friedman and King say the federal government should step in.

The two men would probably differ as to the scope of the payment to eliminate poverty versus replacing a "living wage."

At what income level is poverty over? What income level should the government guarantee? The poverty threshold is probably too small to be labeled a living wage. Most Americans would think a living wage, a level of income more comfortable to live, is closer to two times the poverty threshold.[20] A comparison follows:

	Poverty Threshold	2X poverty Threshold
One Person household	$12,488	$24,976
Two Person household	$15,877	$31,754
Three Person household	$19,515	$39,030
Four Person household	$25,094	$50,188
Five Person household	$29,714	$59,428
Six Person household	$33,618	$67,236

The challenge is that there are 39.7 million Americans below the poverty threshold. But there are an additional 56.0 million below two times the poverty threshold.[21] It is one thing to move all Americans out of poverty and quite another to move them and 56.0 million more Americans to an income level equivalent to a living wage.

The poverty gap totaled $178 billion in 2017 — the amount necessary to move all people to a level of income equaling the poverty threshold. This would solve the poverty problem.[22] The Living Wage Gap, however, totals approximately $800 billion a year, the cost to move all Americans to a level of income equivalent to two times the poverty threshold, or a level approximating a living wage.[23] Such a government program would be one of the largest programs in the federal government, as big as the defense budget and almost twice as large as Medicaid. It would be well over twice as high as the entire welfare budget today, which covers such programs as SNAP (food stamps), Housing Assistance, EITC, SSI, Pell Grants, Child Nutrition, TANF and other programs.[24]

It's hard to imagine that a living wage program would be adopted by the federal government anytime in the foreseeable future. The welfare programs that exist today trigger a political debate that is emotional and polarized. Conservatives feel billions of dollars have been spent on welfare with little success in lowering poverty, with the unintended consequence of the reliance on welfare and a reduction in personal responsibility. Progressives feel that welfare has helped cover the inadequacies of the free market system, and that more money should be spent to help those who have been left behind by the system.

Let's break down the arguments further.

Here are the arguments for social justice and income redistribution: There is too much wealth held by the top 1% in America, and those at the bottom of the income scale have poorly paying jobs or no jobs at all through no fault of their own. Capitalism has failed, and the only solution is to have government take from the rich and give to the poor. In the end many progressives call for much higher taxes on the rich and the redistribution of wealth to lower-income Americans to achieve a living wage for all.

Here are the arguments for a free economy and personal responsibility: In the end the only tried-and-true worldwide solution to wealth generation is the free market and a growing economy, which lifts everyone. Communism and socialism always fail in the end to establish a strong economy and a large middle class. Conservatives feel the problems in America today are from too much regulation and high taxes. And if we were to implement a large redistribution program, the economy would be crushed, jobs would be lost and more people would be worse off.

Chances are that you side with one set of the arguments above. The nation seems to be split right down the middle as it relates to the issue. Do you believe that government can solve the problem or would it only make things worse? It pretty much comes down to that. So what do we do now? Where do we go from here?

I believe we need to skip over the political debate and jump to the practical conclusion: For the foreseeable future, measured in decades, the U.S. is not going to adopt a guaranteed income at a level equaling a living wage. Said another way, in at least the next 10 years, the nation will not adopt laws to establish income redistribution that achieves a minimum of two times the poverty threshold for all Americans.

Consider the following:

- A living wage for the 40 million people in poverty and the additional 56 million below two times the poverty level (which is closer to a living wage) would be an enormous government program twice as large as the entire welfare system and as large as the defense budget.

- In eight years of progressive policy under the Obama administration, the first two of which had a democratic, filibuster-proof majority in the Senate and a strong majority in the House, nothing approximating a "living wage" was passed. It wasn't even seriously debated. The largest income-redistribution policy change under Obama was Obamacare, which helped several million people get a subsidy for their health insurance — small potatoes compared to a living wage.

- Tax laws may change, minimum-wage laws may be enacted, existing programs such as SNAP or health care might be expanded, but these are a far cry from a guaranteed income equaling a living wage.

- Americans have a strong commitment to work. In a recent poll, 87% of Americans favor a work requirement as a condition for receiving welfare.[25] The problem is there is no support to create a large and expensive government program, dwarfing anything we have today, to redistribute income at a level equivalent to a living wage.

The glaring fact is that if you are in poverty waiting on the government for a living wage, you are going to be waiting a long time. The same is true if you wait for help from charities, because there isn't enough horsepower to distribute enough benefits to achieve the standard of a living wage. All charitable giving in the U.S. totaled $358 billion in 2014, of which half went to educational and religious institutions.[26] This takes us to the third postulate.

POSTULATE 3

A guaranteed income approaching a living wage will not be enacted in the U.S. for the foreseeable future. Those in poverty may get help through government programs and charity, but they will achieve a living wage only if they earn it, or at least a large part of it, themselves.

This is not a call to abandon government policy or disbar charities. Just the opposite. We need both government and charities to help tackle the poverty problem. (In an upcoming chapter, I will propose ideas to achieve that.) Instead, this is a wake-up call to Americans to realize that government and charities will not solve the problem alone. We need a plan to solve poverty without over-reliance on government and charities.

The good news is that such a plan exists. But it's buried deep in all the poverty noise. It is a plan that works 98% of the time.

6

LIFE SKILLS

Call it blaming the victim if you like, but decisions made by individuals are paramount in the fight to reduce poverty and increase opportunity in America. The nation's struggle to expand opportunity will continue to be an uphill battle if young people do not learn to make better decisions about their future.

— *Ron Haskins, The Brookings Institution* [27]

What if we had a plan to solve our poverty crisis? What if the plan worked 98% of the time? Wouldn't that be great? That is exactly what Ron Haskins and Isabel Sawhill from The Brookings Institution had. It caused quite a stir and went all the way to a congressional hearing. No one knew quite what to do with it. Actually, it wasn't really a plan per se, it was more of a target statistic. A very simple statistic. They looked at Census reports and other data and concluded that people had only a 2% chance of being in poverty if they did three things:

1. Complete at least a high school education

2. Work full time

3. Wait until age 21 and get married before having a baby.[28]

Isabel Sawhill of The Brookings Institution   *Ron Haskins of The Brookings Institution*

The statistic was both surprising and intuitive. Surprising because we think that poverty is more complicated than that. We think that you can have all of those things and it isn't enough. But it does work for most people. If everyone in America had the three things, then only 2% of the population would be in poverty instead of the 12.3% who are in poverty today.

Intuitive because you could hear your grandfather explaining the three things: telling you why an education is important, why marriage is valuable or how obtaining a work ethic is an essential personal trait. He wouldn't think the three things are all that revolutionary. To his generation they were basic life skills everyone needed to master.

But today we've lost touch with the basics. Perhaps because too many of us were never taught them to begin with or grew up where survival was the day-to-day goal, not education or work ethic. Perhaps there are no jobs out there and therefore no way to work. Perhaps homelessness, crime or drugs bury the three things in irrelevancy. There are lots of reasons why we have lost the basics, but the harsh reality is that we had better find them. They are our best hope in the fight against poverty — actually the only hope. We have concluded that the only way for Americans to get a living wage is to earn it — or at least earn a large portion of it. So life skills are the key to winning the fight against poverty.

No matter what your political persuasion, it is unrealistic to pretend that government or charity will cure poverty in America. Only the individuals in poverty can do that. They can get help along the way, but they must accomplish the three basic skills if they want to get out of poverty and obtain a living wage. It's as simple as that. If they have missed the third trait, then they are going to have to work extra hard on the first and second. One hopes that government programs, charities and caring people can help, but if Americans truly want to leave poverty behind, they will ultimately have to solve the problem themselves.

That is the harsh reality our grandfathers knew. Maybe that is why they were big believers in education, work ethic and marriage.

It's also important to say that not all people in poverty lack life skills. We know that many have a tremendous work ethic and many are well-educated. The critical point is that without life skills, it is very difficult to climb out of the poverty pit.

Choices

America is the land of the free. Adults have the opportunity to do what they want and make their own choices. We have free will unless we break the law. Freedom comes with a price, and that price is that choices have consequences. Good choices help people progress; bad ones set them back.

Good choices help us gain life skills — skills necessary to acquire an education, work ethic and a moral core. Such life skills are a prerequisite for people to get themselves out of poverty. But such life skills are often lost if there is no parental involvement. That unfortunate fact tells us what we are up against.

In sum, no matter what their station in life, their history, or the unfairness of it all, the impoverished must acquire life skills, and we ought to help them make good decisions to get there. Otherwise they will remain in poverty. And that is unacceptable. We have only one route to go.

POSTULATE #4

POSTULATE 4

For those in poverty we need to support, teach and mentor life skills. We must also teach them a work ethic and moral consciousness. Without life skills people in poverty will never earn a living wage and gain financial independence. And we must help them avoid bad decisions.

That is something that few of our charities and even fewer government programs want to tackle. It's a challenge for all of us to gain life skills, but it can be particularly challenging for impoverished people. As a nation we must help them gain these most valuable traits.

However, many of the poor have good life skills and a strong work ethic. Our goal should be to help those who don't have these skills. To end poverty we also need more jobs available at higher wages. But one postulate at a time.

So how do we help poor people acquire life skills? How should we support the poor? Many of us have a calling to do so. In fact, most Americans want to help. That is why so much is given to charities each year. We do what we can, and most of us feel any contribution is a good thing, right down to giving spare change to a panhandler on the street. We have big hearts. But first we must answer this critical question: Is anything we contribute helpful? Or does it do more harm than good?

7

FIRST DO NO HARM

"Real change, not spare change."

— *Bob Cote, Step Denver charity, Denver, Colorado*

Bob Cote working the street

Bob Cote's story is classic. He was the drunk who one day threw away his half-empty bottle of booze and quit forever. After two years of chronic alcoholism that cost him a good job and his family, Cote found the strength to quit drinking. He hit rock bottom but he wasn't through. He looked at his drunk friend passed out in the gutter and realized that together they were killing each other. He talked several of his friends into stopping drinking. Thus began Cote's mission to save lives.

Cote founded an organization called Step Denver[29] in the heart of downtown Denver. He ran the charity for 30 years until his death in 2013. Hundreds of alcoholics conquered their addiction with the help of Cote and Step Denver. Alcoholics quickly learned that Cote was serious about changing them. But unless they were committed to stop drinking, he wasn't going to help them. Cote was tough but so was the problem he was tackling.

I visited Step Denver in 2011, two years before Cote's death. It didn't take too long to realize how tough a customer he was and how big his heart was. Cote wasn't interested in making life more comfortable for alcoholics; his goal was to tackle the difficult problem of helping them conquer their addiction and change their lives. In Cote's world they had no choice. He knew from personal experience that giving money to a chronic alcoholic enabled the problem. Give them food and housing, and they had the resources to buy booze. By doing so you were "killing them on the installment plan." [30]

Cote insisted alcoholics give up drinking when they came to Step Denver. He tested them often to make sure they were sober. If they stayed off booze, Cote would provide the "hand up — a place to live, three meals a day and job training — but not until then. His program for his clients brought them back to functioning lives by steadily adding work responsibilities. The first job was making coffee in the morning or straightening the chairs in the dining room. And the responsibilities grew from there. As long as the former alcoholic continued to progress, Cote continued to help. But stop working, and Cote gave his aid to the next guy. It was the toughest of love, but in the end it saved hundreds.

Cote's biggest challenge in motivating his clients to want to change was side-stepping charities, government welfare and personal handouts that enabled destructive behavior.

We all know that charity and compassion are virtues — most of us think the more the better. Harm is not something we associate with them. It took Cote to make me realize that compassion is necessary in the giver, but its effectiveness needs to be measured by those receiving our charity.

Compassion and charity are admirable traits. Putting others before self is a godlike quality many of us strive for. Clearly, a society made up of such people is far better than one without.

But as a nation, we spend a great deal on welfare at the state and federal level to protect those less fortunate. As individuals we give generously to charities, and that giving has expanded faster than the U.S. economy over the past 50 years. [31] We have one of the most giving cultures in the world.

But things get a lot more complicated when we look at the mind of the receiver. Is it possible to do more harm than good to the receivers of our charity and compassion?

Most experts agree that giving money to a beggar can result in harm. Speaker and writer Mike Yankoski describes the problem in his book "Under the Overpass: A Journey of Faith on the Streets of America."

Yankoski tells an amazing story. Two college kids lived on the street with no money and no shelter in order to bring attention to homelessness. They spent five months wandering the streets of six large cities living on handouts and living with homeless people. Here is how Yankoski answered the question, "Should you give money to beggars?"

> We met other homeless men and women whose only income was from money dropped into a hat or cup. Unfortunately, it's also true that a significant portion of the men and women we knew on the streets would — within a half-hour of receiving a donation — spend it entirely on drugs or alcohol. A nugget of marijuana or crack is only five dollars, and a forty-ounce beer is only two-fifty. So your money is probably providing someone with their fix before you even get home or back to the office. That's why I recommend you give something other than cash. [32]

The problem of enabling addiction is not new. Here is an excerpt from A Handbook of Charity Organization, written in 1882 by Rev. S. Humphreys Gurteen:

> It is a sad fact, but a fact nevertheless, that a great deal of the drunkenness which existed among the poorer classes, was found to be attributable to the money which Christian people had been in the habit of giving in the sacred name of charity. Of this fact the Society had abundant proof. [33]

Economist Nicholas Eberstadt, Commentary Magazine

Alcohol abuse and drug addiction is a growing problem that has reached epidemic proportions. It's a problem we can't ignore. A powerful article titled "Our Miserable 21st Century,"[34] written by economist Nicholas Eberstadt, cites statistics that will make you cringe. Quoting Eberstadt,

In the fall of 2016, Alan Krueger, former chairman of the President's Council of Economic Advisers, released a study that further reflected the picture of the real existing opioid epidemic in America: According to his work, nearly half of all prime working-age male labor-force dropouts — an army now totaling roughly 7 million men — currently take pain medication on a daily basis.

By 2013, according to a 2015 report by the Drug Enforcement Administration, more Americans died from drug overdoses (largely but not wholly opioid abuse) than from either traffic fatalities or guns.

A short but electrifying 2015 paper by Anne Case and Nobel Economics Laureate Angus Deaton talked about a mortality trend that had gone almost unnoticed until then: rising death rates for middle-aged U.S. whites. By Case and Deaton's reckoning, death rates rose somewhat slightly over the 1999–2013 period for all non-Hispanic white men and women 45-54 years of age — but they rose sharply for those with high school diplomas or less, and for this less-educated grouping, most of the rise in death rates was accounted for by suicides, chronic liver cirrhosis and poisonings (including drug overdoses).

Health has been deteriorating for a significant swath of white America in our new century, thanks in large part to drug and alcohol abuse. All this sounds a little too close for comfort to the story of modern Russia, with its devastating vodka and drug-binging health setbacks. Welcome to our new America.

In sum, too many Americans are affected by alcohol and drug addiction.

Clearly, we have not come to grips with how to treat people with alcohol and drug addiction in our public policy. Compassion and handouts are only Band-Aid solutions. We need to know where our money is going and what it's accomplishing. Anything short of that has the possibility of doing more harm than good.

A Handbook on Charity Organization succinctly addresses the issue: "While real charity has a beatitude attached to it, there is no such blessing promised to the man who gives only for the selfish pleasure it affords, the good name it purchases or the annoyance it prevents." [35]

POSTULATE 5

We must exercise effective compassion in the dealing with those that are suffering from alcoholism or addiction to drugs. We must not enable destructive behavior with donations of money.

Tackling poverty

Critical question: Can we do more harm than good by distributing money or benefits from charity and welfare programs to the impoverished even if they don't have addiction problems? I wish the answer to that question were a resounding no. But after working with the poor and studying welfare, I've come to the conclusion that the answer is too often yes. Too often we enable bad acts, bad decisions and dependency. It's time to look at what we are doing with great care and thought.

8

THE RISK OF DEPENDENCY

To relieve the misfortunes of our fellow creatures is concurring with the Deity; 'tis godlike; but if we provide encouragement for laziness, and supports for folly, may it not be found fighting against the order of God and Nature, which perhaps has appointed want and misery as the proper punishments for, and cautions against as well as necessary consequences of idleness and extravagancy? Whenever we attempt to amend the scheme of Providence, and to interfere with the government of the world, we had need be very circumspect lest we do more harm than good.

— *Benjamin Franklin* [36]

Pastor Susan Lyon of Care Placement Services

A man and his wife living day-to-day were among our first clients seeking temporary housing. At the time I was working for a newly created nonprofit employment agency called Care Placement Services (CPS).

A day after opening our doors, we got a job interview for the man. It fit his skills perfectly. To our surprise he never showed up for the interview. Instead he had gone to help his son work on a truck. Now we had egg on our face, which didn't bother him much. Over the next few weeks, we tried in vain to get him to go back to work.

We quit trying. I wish I could say this was an isolated incident, but it was more the rule than the exception in our newly formed organization. In fact, of the first 40 people in the door, we didn't place a single one of them in a job. And that was not because they had no skills or that there were no jobs out there. We could have gotten jobs for every one of them. So what was wrong?

The head of CPS was Pastor Susan Lyon, a very skilled employment match-maker. She formed CPS because she wanted to address the root problem of poverty — unemployment. She had great connections with employers and was a skilled counselor in teaching interview skills and writing résumés. But she also had a big heart — one that could come only from personal experience.

But life has a way of pitching unexpected curve balls.

On a spring day, April 28, 1982, Lyon's life was changed forever. She was hit by a passing truck while walking along a road in North Denver. She nearly died and probably should have. A doctor at the hospital attributed her recovery to divine intervention, which actually made it into the hospital records. Lyon says that was the day her life serving Christ began. After eight months Lyon left the hospital. Having to support two boys, ages three and nine, as a single parent, Lyon had her work cut out for her. Her husband had abandoned her after the accident because he didn't want to be married to someone with heavy financial burdens and physical disabilities. During that difficult time, Lyon was supported solely by friends. But it was hardly enough to live on. Her disabilities prevented her from returning to a well-paying job. Compounding her problems, she was unable to get public assistance.

But Lyon was a fighter, determined to put her life back together. After much thought she came up with the idea of putting her prior experience in job place-ment to good use by starting an employment service. But with a new twist. Lyon focused on finding jobs for people who, like herself, faced hardships, many of which they had no control over. She adopted the axiom, "If you work for God, God will work for you."

Over time Lyon became a pastor and opened a ministry in Denver, which also serves as a food bank and boarding house. She also offers support services for the poor.

She has helped hundreds of people get back on their feet. In 2014 when she was looking for help to fund CPS, I was happy to lend a hand getting her charity off the ground. We raised about $20,000 to kick off a new employment agency to serve the poor.

Most charities stop short of actually finding jobs for people. Instead they provide résumé help, interview support and career counseling. We were determined to go all the way and help impoverished people get jobs — the Holy Grail of poverty.

We had five volunteers and enough money to do the basics. We rented an office, created a website and began marketing our services. Two months later, we had 40 clients but no success finding them jobs.

What was the problem?

In our first board meeting after opening our doors. we met to discuss the problem. It was an intense conversation with diverse views, but in the end we all agreed on one point — the people we had counseled didn't really want a job. They talked a good game, but they were really after something else — free handouts, such as food or bus passes, or confirmation of their job searches to continue their unemployment benefits. We surmised that the reasons they were not serious about employment were varied and included the following:

- Low wages

- Adversity to work

- Unrealistic job expectations

- Dependency on welfare or charity

- Addiction to drugs or alcohol

The surprising thing was that employers were very receptive to our plans and shared plenty of job opportunities with us. They desperately needed help but could not find good employees. They explained that too many people didn't know how to work or would do a good job, but then a problem would arise, and they would not come back to work. It could be as complex as drugs or alcohol or as simple as a broken-down car. As a new employment agency, we wanted to bridge that gap. We wanted to go the extra mile to help people with the challenges in their lives — housing, food and clothes, to name a few — and put them in a stable work environment. Our intensions were good, and as an organization we were working hard. But something wasn't right. We were zero for 40, and that hurt.

Like so many in the charity world we wanted our compassion to be enough. But it wasn't. More important than our goal were our clients' goals. The above issue is a common problem of working with the poor. The culture in which we seek to deliver help often overwhelms our ability to help. Once we recognized the problem, we focused on those we could help, those who truly wanted a job. We realized that we could offer jobs, but we couldn't persuade anyone to take them. We would be open to help but only those who truly wanted help would get our attention. We found a way to focus our volunteers on clients who really wanted to go back to work. We refocused ourselves, and after our first year in business, these were our statistics:

- Total individuals who came to CPS for inquiries into jobs: 548

- Clients who went through the CPS interview and assessment process: 286

- Clients who found a job on their own aided by employment counseling: 136

- Clients placed in a job by CPS counselors: 43

In the end we raised and spent about $20,000 and found 43 jobs, equating to about $500 per job found. From my perspective, these are pretty good numbers in the poverty and welfare world. That $500 went a long way in establishing economic health for the worker and community. Still, it breaks my heart that so many we talked with did not go back to work. I didn't understand why but I knew that is the wrong direction for our nation and for those in poverty.

After much study I learned that I had to confront one of the oldest problems facing the poverty issue. Our collective welfare, charity and personal efforts push some people down and zap their initiative. They are not interested in work, instead maneuvering through the welfare and charity system for food and benefits. Unfortunately jobs at low wages don't interest them, even though it means an improvement to their lives and a steppingstone to financial independence. What is this phenomenon, and how can we reverse its influence?

As you study the problem, it becomes immediately apparent it is as old as poverty itself. Today we call the problem "dependency," meaning people become dependent on welfare and charity and avoid self-sufficiency. A century ago they would call it the pauperization of the poor. Pauperize means to reduce to poverty[37]. *A Handbook of Charity Organization*, mentioned earlier, opened its introduction with this: [38]

> There is scarcely any one of the great problems affecting the public good which has taken as strong a hold upon the national mind of Europe, or indeed upon the minds of the more intelligent portion of our own people, as the question of the prevention of the pauperization of the poor.
>
> It is a question which has been discussed in almost every civilized country in the world. Statesmen, clergymen and philanthropists have approached the problem from various sides. It has been studied theoretically; it has been handled practically; it has occupied

the attention of legislative bodies; it has been made the subject of platform oratory; and it has forced its way into the daily press, the reviews and the magazines. It has been experimented upon by devoted men and devoted women in the crowded city and in the secluded hamlet. It a word, it has been, for years past, one of the leading questions of the day.

Indeed. That was in 1882, and we have spent 136 years since it was written trying to answer the question. We introduced the federal government to the fight with an elaborate and expensive welfare system. We lived through the Great Depression, the Great Society, welfare reform, various state programs and the creation of thousands of charities. Presidents have grappled with the problem, congresses with Democratic and Republican control have fought the problem, and still the question seems as elusive as ever.

The problem is dependency or pauperization — the fact that our welfare and charity systems can push people down instead of building them up. We have been ignoring this problem for too long, and yet we know a fair amount about it. We have an extensive history in America and Europe coping with charity and welfare, and we can learn from our history. Here is what Benjamin Franklin had to say about the English welfare system in 1766:

> I am for doing good to the poor, but I differ in opinion of the means.—I think the best way of doing good to the poor, is not making them easy *in* poverty, but leading or driving them *out* of it. In my youth I travelled much, and I observed in different countries, that the more public provisions were made for the poor, the less they provided for themselves, and of course became poorer. And, on the contrary, the less was done for them, the more they did for themselves, and became richer. There is no country in the world [but England] where so many provisions are established for them; so many hospitals to receive them when they are sick or lame, founded and maintained by voluntary charities; so many alms-houses for the aged of both sexes, together with a solemn general law made by the rich to subject their estates to a heavy tax for the support of the poor. Under all these obligations, are our poor modest, humble, and thankful; and do they use their best endeavors to maintain themselves, and lighten our shoulders of this burthen?—On the contrary, I affirm that there is no country in the world in which the poor are more idle, dissolute, drunken, and insolent.

The day you passed that act, you took away from before their eyes the greatest of all inducements to industry, frugality, and sobriety, by giving them a dependence on somewhat else than a careful accumulation during youth and health, for support in age or sickness. In short, you offered a premium for the encouragement of idleness, and you should not now wonder that it has had its effect in the increase of poverty. Repeal that law, and you will soon see a change in their manners.[39]

Benjamin Franklin

The English relief system created a pauperized class that was difficult to motivate and change. That is exactly the same problem faced by CPS. What we experienced is that low wages combined with poor life skills and often dependency on handouts and welfare is a dysfunctional brew. If that sounds like blaming the victim, I didn't intend that. But I can't ignore that fact that CPS had jobs for the taking and many folks did not want them.

Nor am I alone. Here are comments from Robert D. Lupton, author of the book *Toxic Charity*:

> In the United States, there's a growing scandal that we both refuse to see and actively perpetuate. What Americans avoid facing is that while we are very generous in charitable giving, much of that money is either wasted or actually harms the people it is targeted to help. I don't say this casually or cavalierly. I have spent over four decades working in inner-city Atlanta and beyond, trying to develop models of urban renewal that are effective and truly serve the poor. There is nothing that brings me more joy than seeing

people transitioned out of poverty, or neighborhoods change from being described as "dangerous" and "blighted" to being called "thriving" and even "successful." I have worked with churches, government agencies, entrepreneurs, and armies of volunteers and know from firsthand experience the many ways that "good intentions" can translate into ineffective care or even harm.[40]

I believe that our federal and state governments and many of our charities operate based on free handouts and this has caused a culture of dependency that is pervasive. I think we have taken the pride and worth away from many of the poor and in effect communicated to them that we will take care of them with the unintended consequence of telling them they can't, or don't need to do so themselves. I think we have inadvertently established too many of the poor as nonparticipants in our communities. This isn't just a government problem; many of our charities and churches are guilty of the same thing. In fact it was charities and churches in America that faced the problem in the 1800s prior to government being involved in any way.

POSTULATE
#6

POSTULATE 6

We must practice effective compassion in the granting of benefits from government or charity to make sure we are pulling people up to self-sufficiency and not pushing them down to dependency.

This postulate is probably the most controversial of those proposed in the book. But I understand that they are fighting words to others. It isn't worth fighting over, because if we jump to how to fix things, we could all get excited about that. I believe we can skip right by the culture, the cause and the history and focus on the change. We can move past words like dependency and personal responsibility and get right into change. Change, well-thought-through and balanced, would excite us all, even those who think I am wrong about this.

In the end we could get more resources to the poor, giving them more flexibility and responsibility. We could reignite the passion of Americans to help those in need, at the same time improve the economic health of the nation. If all that sounds too good be true, remember that we spend billions on charity and welfare and thousands of hours as social workers and volunteers. Unfortunately, much of it disjointed and ineffective. We have a lot of resources to work with, and if it was coordinated, it would yield powerful results.

We could change the culture by adding hope, worth and pride. It wouldn't be fake or prescribed. The poor have much to offer our nation, and it is time to realize that both in theory and practice. So let's establish some macro solutions in the next three chapters and get some detailed plans for implementation in the four chapters after that.

On the macro scale, there are three things we must do to fix welfare and charities. All three of them are from lessons learned in the past. They are 1) we must know who we are helping and what we are trying to do on a person-by-person basis (discern); 2) we must make sure that those we are helping want to be helped (buy-in); and 3) as we help people, they must help the community and themselves (something for something).

These simple rules are not too harsh, but they would revolutionize the charity and welfare world and help us help people. They are based on principles we have learned over the years but have stopped practicing.

We can't go on dealing with poverty, welfare and charity in the same blind way. For too long we have not faced up to the problems and learned from the past. It is frustrating knowing that today we face the same problems with poverty faced 136 years ago. In 1882 *A Handbook on Charity Organization* had the following conclusion regarding the English system of relief:

> By making no distinction between the deserving and the undeserving, no attempt to discover and remove the causes of distress, it was actually corrupting the morals and swallowing up the resources of the country. [41]

Isn't that exactly the problem we face today?

9

DISCERNMENT

But merely responding with a "relief check" to complicated social or personal problems — such as ill health, faulty education, domestic discord, racial discrimination, or inadequate skills — is not likely to provide a lasting solution.

— *President John F. Kennedy* [42]

The patient, referred to as Pamela C [43], had been brought in 49 times over several years to the psychiatric emergency room of the hospital for care. She was a homeless woman with schizophrenia. When she quit taking her medication, she started mutilating herself. First she cut off her fingers. She was brought in for treatment, put back on medication to control her schizophrenia and then was released to the streets after she promised she would stay on her medication. But she never did and eventually she began mutilating herself again until she had no fingers, toes, tongue, eyelids or ears. If that sounds like something that could never happen in a civilized nation like ours, think again. It happened in Los Angeles.

The incident and many more are described in *Street Crazy* by Stephen B. Seager, M.D., a psychiatrist who worked in a large county hospital in Los Angeles. It is a haunting and powerful book about mental illness and homelessness. Seager experienced the problems firsthand, and his book is a call for change to fix a dysfunctional system. The problem begins with the issue of many of our homeless population suffering various degrees of mental illness, some of them quite serious.

Makeup of Adult Homeless Population in 25 American Cities

- 28% severely mentally ill
- 22% physically disabled
- 18% were employed
- 15% victims of domestic violence
- 13% veterans
- 3% HIV Positive

Because these are not mutually exclusive characteristics, the same person may appear in multiple categories.

Seager's opinion was supported by the Conference of Mayors of 25 large American cities. The Conference releases a report every year of statistics of homelessness, as shown to the left.[44]

Seager asserts two very interesting facts about the mental illness problem. First is that most mental illness experienced by the homeless fit one of three types — major depression, bipolar disorder and schizophrenia. Second is that the treatment of these diseases has made great advances over the past 25 years.

Seager points out that mental illness is a disease affecting the brain, and we need to think of it the same way we would any disease affecting the body. We can diagnose the disease and treat it, and patients can often return to productive, normal lives.

But one of the problems with treatment is that once patients are no longer suffering from the disease, many believe they don't need to be on the drugs, experience their side effects or pay for them. They stop taking the medicine, and once they stop, the disease returns. As long as they are not violent to anyone but themselves, there is nothing the police or loved ones can do.

The worst case is that an accident or injury happens, and the person ends up back in the hospital, put back on the drugs and stabilized again. Actually that's often the best-case scenario. The worst is when the person ends up back on the street, barely surviving and living a life of destitution, beyond the reach of loved ones to help.

It is not hard to find these people — they make up the majority of the mentally ill homeless population as documented in the Conference of Mayors' report.

How is this possible in America? It stems from our love and respect for freedom. Most state laws respect the freedom of people over 18 years old to live the life they want. The homeless mentally ill are protected by the courts to wander the streets as long as they are not harmful to anyone but themselves. Pamela C had the legal right to use the psychiatric hospital 49 times to cut herself to pieces.

It wasn't always this way in America. In the 1950s anyone with a mental illness usually landed in a state institution and spent his or her life there. They were often horrible places. The care was often poor, because the state hospitals were woefully underfunded. It's no surprise the hospitals were dirty, neglected and understaffed. That changed in the 1960s, when many of the nonviolent patients were returned to the community. Sadly, many had no place to go but the streets.[45] This was done in order to give back freedom to the mentally ill who were not a threat to anyone but themselves. The irony of the situation is that doing so has condemned many with a debilitating illness to a life on the streets. Today, they might be cured by new drugs and treatments not available in the 1950s.

The other point about the homeless mentally ill is that they exist beyond the reach of the federal safety net. Most programs, such as SNAP, miss these folks. The welfare system can't deal with transient people with no wherewithal to receive electronic benefit cards for food or vouchers for rent.

It is a tragedy that those most in need are missed because they fall right through the safety net. They are a sad picture of desperation, an example of how the poor are desperately in need of more resources. Over 50 years we have expanded the safety net on numerous occasions, but the homeless and most desperate are not helped. It is a travesty and nothing short of immoral. We hold the homeless up as examples and then spend the money elsewhere, often on those with income above the poverty threshold. It won't change until we come up with a way to balance freedom with the moral obligation to intercede to halt a disease. That is a most difficult balance to strike.

It is easier to turn a blind eye on the mentally ill and ignore the problem. We keep a distance and act as if we are afraid of them rather than cure them. Why? Rather than allocate resources to understand them, which precedes a cure, we shun them. In politically correct America, this is morally and ethically wrong.

Let's back up and remember our goals.

- A hand up not merely a hand out.

- Simplifying the Chinese proverb mentioned earlier, "Teach a man to fish, and you feed him for a lifetime."

- Help people gain their financial independence.

Considering that the above are our goals, we can conclude only that most of our charitable and welfare programs are wholly inadequate. For the bulk of our charity and welfare programs, we don't even attempt to achieve our goal. Take food as an example. In the United States we have hundreds of food banks and soup kitchens. At the federal level we have SNAP and other food programs that distribute billions in electronic payment cards and vouchers for the purchase of food. Giving away food is the goal of these charities and government programs, and success is measured by how much food is given away. Most of the time those handing out food don't even know the people they are giving it to. There is little focus on helping people become food independent. Why do we stop short?

We stop short because we think people know how to fish; they just don't have fish right now. More specifically, there are just not enough jobs that pay a living wage. We assume everyone knows how to work and has the necessary education and life skills to get good jobs. This kind of thinking is not a justification for assuming everything is OK and not looking deeper. We know that often something is lacking in the individuals or families. It could be inadequate education, poor life skills or something more invasive like addiction or mental illness. We can't just assume everyone knows how to fish or we will never help anyone learn to fish. That is morally wrong. In short, families need help.

Some would argue that an insensitive free enterprise system is far more to blame for poverty than the individuals experiencing it. That is an interesting observation and may or may not be true, but it is hardly the reason not to teach a man to fish. We are not trying to lay blame here but trying to figure out whether the person knows how to fish or not. We can teach a man to fish without laying blame. It is a good reminder to strive to teach with love in our hearts and the best interest of the receiver in mind. Most charities have such standards.

The real reason we don't teach people how to fish is that we are afraid to get personal. The prevailing logic is that it is not our business to judge the poor because it is simply not appropriate. But we can't have it both ways. We can't believe in teaching and fixing problems and yet be afraid to discern the level of expertise of the person we seek to help.

When we teach a man to fish we are in effect saying, "You don't know how to fish; I know how to fish; let me teach you how to fish." This doesn't happen unless we discern that the person doesn't know how and needs to know how. We do so with a desire to help and we don't blame the individual for not knowing how to fish. After all, we didn't know how to fish until someone taught us how. Isn't that true with all life skills?

Of course it gets a lot more complicated in the real world where life skills regarding work ethic, employment, savings, budgeting, cooking and raising children are necessary for economic freedom. That makes discernment a challenge and judging much more personal. So we don't do it, because it is much easier to just give away food and leave it at that.

Why our interaction with the poor has come to this is odd. Such thinking does not exist in education. We readily test the knowledge of students, for example. It doesn't exist in sports. We assess the skill level of athletes, find their weaknesses and attempt to strengthen them. Nor does it exist with business managers. We try to understand the skill level of their employees so they can help them improve. But in the world of poverty, this kind of thinking is nonexistent.

In the end such thinking is responsible for successful people's failure to disseminate their vast experience to those in need. The reasons for not teaching life skills are apathy and insensitivity. When we say, "Oh it isn't my job to judge the poor," what we are really saying is, "Here is a fish; come back and get another one tomorrow." When we say it is not our responsibility to judge the poor, we are condemning the mentally ill living on our streets, struggling with a disease that together we might be able to cure.

If we want to achieve our goals, we have to embrace discernment. In 1882 they also were fighting the desire to "give asking no questions." Here is an observation from *A Handbook of Charity Organization*:

> In Every Christian country in which *"give and ask no questions"* has usurped the place of Scriptural and rational alms-giving, what has been the result? We need not instance so flagrant an example of that of Christian Italy, which is overrun with Pauperism. Take the case of Christian Belgium. In Brussels, one out of every eight of its inhabitants is the recipient of relief; at Bruges one in three; at Tournai one-half of the entire population. [46]

POSTULATE
#7

POSTULATE 7

Charities, welfare officials and mentors must embrace discernment as the first step in solving poverty. Without it we are simply handing out food and clothing, for example, and expecting those in need to climb the socioeconomic ladder without personal attention or help. Everyone needs guidance and help learning life skills, and it is unfair to expect those in poverty to succeed alone.

President John F. Kennedy

President Kennedy summed up the problem eloquently in a speech to Congress in 1962:

> Today, in a year of relative prosperity and high employment, we are more concerned about the poverty that persists in the midst of abundance. The reasons are often more social than economic, more often subtle than simple. Some are in need because they are untrained for work — some because they cannot work, because they are too young or too old, blind or crippled. Some are in need because they are discriminated against for reasons they cannot help. Responding to their ills with scorn or suspicion is inconsistent with our moral precepts and inconsistent with their nearly universal preference to be independent. But merely responding with a "relief check" to complicated social or personal problems — such as ill health, faulty education, domestic discord, racial discrimination, or inadequate skills — is not likely to provide a lasting solution. Such a check must be supplemented, or in some cases made unnecessary, by positive services and solutions, offering the total resources of the community to meet the total needs of the family to help our less fortunate citizens help themselves.[47]

A Handbook of Charity Organization describes a philosophy from Emmanuel Bailly, the editor of the *Tribune Catholique*, who had taken a fatherly interest in a group of young enthusiasts working with the poor. In 1830 Bailly explains how alms to the poor is not enough; instead we need the "alms of good advice."[48] What a great term.

"If you intend," he said, "the work to be really efficacious; if you are in earnest about serving the poor, you must not let it be a mere doling out of alms, bringing each your pittance of money or food; you must make it a medium of *moral* assistance, you must give them the *alms of good advice*."

Then speaking of the poor, he said, "their one idea, when they fall into distress, is to hold out their hand for an alms, a system which generally proves as ineffectual as it is demoralizing." M. Bailly suggested to his young friends that they should try to remedy this lamentable state of things by placing their education, their intelligence, their special knowledge of law or science, and their general knowledge of life, at the disposal of the poor; that instead of only taking them some little material relief, they should strive to win their confidence, learn all about their affairs, and then see how they could best help them to help themselves."

Bailly is right; if we want to truly have success, we must dole out the alms of good advice, and to do that we need to get to know the individual and the problems they face. The first step in improvement, therefore, has to be discernment. Of course it is hard to focus on improvement if people are hungry or the children are unclothed. We often have to stabilize people's lives before we can focus on improvement, but none of this can happen without discernment. Once we discern the situation, we can work together to overcome the challenges. The key word is *we*. It must be done together, and there is a simple way to make sure that we are on the same page — a simple way to make sure that *we* is really *we*.

10

BUY-IN

You can lead a horse to water but you cannot make it drink.

— *Old English Proverb*

Nobody washes a rented car. That's the ownership adage. It's true; ownership makes all the difference. Taking ownership is also the key to personal improvement and changing our lives. Unless we take ownership of our self-improvement, education or work ethic, not much will happen. "Buy-in" is the prerequisite to success.

It is a simple concept and yet is controversial in charity and welfare. Take the case of a shelter in Denver for battered women. Its leaders encourage the women in their facility to attend counseling sessions. They found that charging the women a nominal fee of $2.50 a session facilitates learning and action. A mere $2.50 a session achieves buy-in for them, and nothing else they have tried is as effective. However the shelter lost an $80,000 government grant because it charges its clients. The grant requires all benefits to be freely distributed. Ultimately the shelter's leaders had to choose between the $2.50 fee or the $80,000 grant. They choose buy-in even though it put them in a financial bind.[49]

Care Placement Service

They chose buy-in because they knew how important it was to the success of their mothers. I lived through the same problem with Care Placement Services (CPS). Buy-in saved CPS. Pastor Susan Lyon formed CPS to function as a non-profit employment agency to help find jobs for those in poverty. But we had experienced no success with the first 40 clients. We had spent considerable time with them, even got them job interviews, but often they wouldn't show up. We learned the hard way that they didn't really want to go back to work even though they never said that. Their actions didn't follow their words. They talked a good game, but they were really after something else — participation in the food bank, a free bus pass or other benefits. We were quite concerned in the first board meeting after forming the organization, working with 40 clients and having no success whatsoever. But Lyon had an idea she was sure would work well to solve our problem. She argued for a "membership fee" to establish buy-in.

We would separate the willing from the unwilling by charging them a $20 membership fee for our services. If they didn't have $20, they could volunteer in the office or for another charity, and we would accept that in payment. For a mere $20, we would find people a job, which is a pretty good deal. Lyon argued that we had to be steadfast in the implementation of the fee. If the client was not willing to pay, then we shouldn't offer help. The $20 would give our clients all of our services including the job search, résumé and interview support, and help with other needs such as housing, clothes and personal hygiene. The $20 served as buy-in to separate those who truly wanted a job from those who wanted something else.

Lyon was adamant about our membership fee. She had lived through this before saying: "You can't help those that don't want to be helped. There are too many people just looking for a freebie." Based on her background those words were particularly poignant.

Lyon had been severely injured as a young mother in a traffic accident and had no means of support. She was helped by family and friends and ultimately by the government safety net. She focused her life on helping the poor. So when she argued for the importance of buy-in, people listened. What she knew from her history and her suffering is that people have to want to help themselves, and without that we are powerless to make a difference in their lives. We can be friendly, pray, hope and nudge, but until buy-in is established, we are not going to make a difference.

So we concluded that we would create the buy-in of $20 and stick to it. Many board members were disappointed that it came to that. We had assumed that our mere presence as mentors armed with jobs and know-how would be enough. Unfortunately, it wasn't. In the charity and welfare world we just assumed that everyone wants to improve his or her life, and nothing else was needed. Unfortunately, we were not on the same page. We didn't know that nothing establishes success better than a simple standard of buy-in. Once invested — even at a small figure of $2.50 to receive services — everyone tries harder.

POSTULATE 8

All of our charities and welfare programs should be based on establishing buy-in as a condition of success. Without it we are just hoping folks would wash a rented car. We would be waiting a long time.

It is a shame that many of our foundations and government grants have moratoriums against charging the poor anything. They equate charging the poor with profiting from the poor. Of course we don't want to profit from the poor, but such a concern is not worth a moratorium on establishing buy-in. Foundations and governments would be far more effective with their dollars if instead of a moratorium on buy-in, they insisted on it. Consideration of buy-in ought to be a key factor in the grant process.

Buy-in can be established through investment in dollars or time, but it must be established. Charities and welfare that don't discern problems and then establish buy-in to fix them will have a slim chance of success. Even with discernment and buy-in, there is one last ingredient necessary for success. When we hand out benefits, we need to hand out pride. But that's tricky. One thing is certain: It doesn't come in a bottle. But we know where it is, and it's time to make it a part of our charity, welfare and mentoring.

||

SOMETHING FOR SOMETHING

Ordinary people sense in their bones both that helping the poor is a priority, and also that the poor must help themselves. Some will ask, how can we do both? If we help the poor, they are not self-reliant, and if they are self-reliant we do not help them. But the two priorities conflict only in political ideology. In local anti-poverty efforts, it is quite possible to combine them.

— *Lawrence Mead* [50]

There is a lot of guilt in America about not doing enough for the poor. Many of us feel guilty when we hear about a child in poverty or read reports about the homeless or downtrodden. And many people feel particularly guilty because they know that the Bible instructs them to help the poor.

Pastor James Forbes summed it up best when he said, "Nobody gets to heaven without a letter of reference from the poor." [51] But we also know that the poor must help themselves. How do we balance these contrasting thoughts?

One day I thought I'd seriously get into the Bible from the perspective of the poor and downtrodden and see what I could learn. So I purchased *The Poverty & Justice Bible*. It was the entire Bible, New and Old Testaments, highlighted with key passages, as described in the foreword by the Rev. Dr. James Lawson: "This is a wonderful Bible in a contemporary rendering, with pertinent passages on poverty and justice highlighted." [52]

Highlighted it was. Nearly every page had something highlighted; 33 highlights in Genesis alone. I knew the Bible had a lot to say about the poor, poverty and justice, but now I was totally overwhelmed. Overlying it all was the push that we should do more. In the middle of the Bible there was a section entitled "The Core," which the publishers had added to highlight their position regarding the poor. It included the following: "We are our brothers' and sisters' keepers, and we love them by serving them. God calls us into community and to be in relationship with him and with one another." [53]

Love them by serving them. I got that point vividly as I read the highlighted sections. But I did not have as vivid a feel for how to help the poor help themselves. Does serving the poor mean helping them to help themselves?

My dilemma came to a head on a mission trip to West Virginia with the youth group from my church. I was a counselor and chaperone of high school kids on a one-week mission trip to repair houses in the Appalachian Mountains. We had taken a bus load of high school students broken up into teams of five students and two adults. We were assigned to our project and introduced to the inhabitants of the house. Our job was to replace a worn-out porch that led to the entrance to their trailer home. Four generations lived in the small trailer. A great-grandmother was cared for by an 18-year-old mother, who also looked after her two-year-old daughter. The middle-aged mom worked full-time as a nurse's assistant.

We were there for a week building the new porch. The place was a mess both inside and out. Not just messy, but unhealthful, with spoiled food in the yard, dirt and dog hair on the floor and stuff piled from floor to ceiling. For five days we worked outside in the heat; all the while the inhabitants stayed inside and watched TV. The baby crawled on the filthy floor covered with dog hair. I know I would not want my kids crawling on a dirty carpet, and it bothered me. It disturbed me even more at the end of the week, when the mother had to take the child to the emergency room with a bad case of hives.

There was plenty of expertise among our volunteers to address the health issues and mentor the inhabitants, but that wasn't our job. Those running the charity had made it clear to us that our job was to work on the house and not comment on the household or its inhabitants. They asked that we not involve ourselves in that way. Our job was to build the porch. As I witnessed serious problems that could be remedied, I wanted to get more involved. But the staff of the charity held firm despite my protests. So I let it go. One evening late in the week, we had a group discussion about compassion and giving with our kids and the charity's staff. The kids raised lots of questions and didn't understand why they were outside working while the family was inside watching TV. I couldn't explain it to them, because I felt the same way. But the leaders of the charity explained that our purpose was to serve and be compassionate with no expectations in return. They explained that that was the highest order of compassion. Don't judge — give. As simple as that.

But I never felt good about it, and I knew many of our kids didn't as well. The executives running the charity were educated professionals, and that was their explanation of what the Bible says is our calling. They questioned our compassion when we raised the issue. My compassion was real, but misunderstood. I'd given a full week of my time, worked my butt off, spent my own money, and after our week in the hot sun, a new sturdy porch was attached to the trailer home. We showed our kids how to be compassionate. They witnessed poverty up close, which many of them had never seen before. Mission accomplished, right? But I couldn't get the household and that two-year-old covered with hives out of my mind. Did the Bible say to put the porch ahead of the health of a two-year-old? Perhaps that wasn't the proper question, but that is how I felt about it then and still do to this day. Was it really none of my business? Is that really the definition of compassion?

After I returned home, I ran across a small book on poverty written by Lawrence Mead. Mead is a professor at New York University and has worked and written about poverty for many years. His book, *From Prophecy to Charity*, was not much bigger than a pamphlet, but I was inspired by it. It had a chapter on poverty and the Bible, which explained the issues so that they made more sense to me and shed some light on my dilemma. Here are some of the quotes that affected me: [54]

> In the New Testament, Like the Old, helping the poor is a priority, but helping means primarily to restore the poor to community rather than simply to subside or liberate them. The community is based on mutual expectations about good behavior.

> Assistance is not a substitute for engagement. The answer to poverty is not redistribution but the rebuilding of relationships with the poor where both sides give and receive.

> Properly understood, the biblical commandment is not to spend more or less on the poor. Rather it is to do what they most require.

Author Lawrence Mead

Based on Mead's biblical interpretation, we missed the most important thing on our mission trip to West Virginia. We did not make the poor women in that household a part of our community. We had lunch with them each day, and we were nice to each other, but we didn't do what they most required. I wish the female adult volunteer had gone into the house and passed along all the wisdom she had — like it was her house and her child. We could have shared housecleaning and health tips. Heck, I'd have brought my vacuum. The 18-year-old should have helped us build the porch, for at least one day. I would have liked to work with her. Perhaps I could have taught her something, and I would have gotten to know her much better. I bet the women of that household would have taught us some things, too. They would have taught us how to live without all the material possessions we think we need in our lives. But that whole human side of things, all that shared community was lost in the instructions to deliver a porch with minimal interface with the occupants. Our job was to deliver compassion with no expectations of any kind. That was explained to me as the highest level of compassion. "Serve and ask nothing in return" is what they said was our charge. They said it is what the Bible instructs.

This is the controversial aspect of compassion versus effective compassion. Much of it seems to be Scripture-based. What seems to come from many of our churches is a calling to serve with no expectations in return. Contrast that to the *Handbook of Charity Organization*.

> The fact is, the trouble does not lie in the Church, still less in Christianity, but in *ourselves* — not in the teaching of the Church, for the Church has never taught her children, as a religious duty, or even as an act of grace, to *give, asking no questions* — the trouble lies in the natural tendency of man to shirk a plain and Scriptural, ay, and arduous duty, and to adopt easy, unchurchly and irrational methods.[55]

The problem is even more prevalent when the debate arises over work and labor expected from the poor. The word used over 100 years ago, "idleness," is almost taboo to talk about today. So is the discussion that many receiving relief became comfortable in that capacity. For many in America, addressing this issue is thought of as totally inappropriate. Yet as we have concluded that without a base level of life skills including a work ethic, the poor will never get out of poverty. Life skills and obtaining a work ethic are not easy to learn, and most of us had help and motivation to achieve success. Why do we refuse to help those in poverty achieve it? Why are we afraid even to address it?

That was at the heart of my dismay on the mission trip. We had our kids outside in the hot sun for five days building a porch. The 18-year-old in the house watched TV all day. Obviously her work ethic was not what it should be. We worked with our kids who did not want to spend that much time in the hot son (truth be told, neither did I), teaching them how to work hard all day. We taught them how to stay hydrated, how to use tools, how to work as a team and how to take pride in their work. It was only a week, but at the end, they were proud of the work they had accomplished. I worried what our presence was indirectly teaching the 18-year-old in the trailer. Did she learn that somehow she is not expected to do such work, or is incapable of such work or that she was happy to have a new porch and pleased to have avoided the work? Or maybe those thoughts never entered her mind. Instead all that happened was that we missed an opportunity for a real encounter of the middle class with the poverty class. I don't know for sure, but my gut says that whatever happened, we didn't really make much progress in the war on poverty during that week. Unless you count the new, very strong porch, which I think will outlast the trailer.

Here is how the *Handbook of Charity Organization"* addresses labor and work:

> Is it, we ask, a very hard-headed thing for the public to require an equivalent of labor, from those who are able to give it, in return for the relief which they receive? It is unchristian? Is in not in the sweat of his brow that man is to eat his bread? Is not the Commandment, "Six days shalt thou labor?" And does not the apostle lay it down as a law, that "if any will not work, neither shall he eat?" And what gives these words peculiar force in this connection, is the fact that when St. Paul penned this command, he was actually speaking of charitable relief and forbids the churches to assist the will-fully idle from the contributions of the faithful. [56]

The reference regarding the Apostle Paul comes from 2 Thessalonians 3:6–15. I wondered what *The Poverty & Justice Bible* did with that reference and was shocked by what I found. It was not highlighted at all. Instead it was skipped as if it did not exist. That amazed me. Two other passages of 2 Thessalonians were highlighted, and the whole chapter is only two pages long.

This is the heart of the problem we face today. The poor will never get out of poverty without life skills and a work ethic. Period. It won't happen, and yet addressing this fact is almost always ignored — pushed aside by political correctness and fear. I do not want to imply that all of those in poverty are lazy. Far from it. Some in poverty work far harder than many in the middle class, and they often work at back-breaking jobs. *The Poverty & Justice Bible* argues that we must find a way to increase earnings for these folks. But that does not mean that all of those in poverty have good life skills and a strong work ethic. When we find that idleness is a problem, we should not be afraid to address it.

I think there is an easy solution to this problem, and its one that we should encourage for welfare and charitable giving. We should get "something for something." Most of the time we give "something for nothing." Our welfare programs and many of our charities seek nothing in return for the aid they administer. There are two problems with something for nothing: 1. It does not put the mentor in a position to work on that which is most required; and 2. It indirectly tells the poor they have nothing that is necessary to contribute. Pure handouts tell the poor they are different from the rest of us. They are worth our stuff but not our time, attention and care. That is certainly no way to raise a child, coach a team, manage a department or teach a class, and it is no way to interact with those we want to help. It wounds pride.

For a solid week in West Virginia, I worked alongside the five teenagers on my team. We sweated together, learned together and talked together. During the week, the 18-year-old in the house remained glued to her TV. She had no male in her family, no one working with her directly. What did we communicate to her indirectly — that the kids I bought, our kids, were worth my time but she was not? What if we had arranged that for a couple of hours each day she needed to find the time to work with us? Or perhaps she should have worked inside the home with some of our team to get it cleaned and organized. Maybe she should have taught our kids how to take care of her grandmother. Any of that would have meant she did something for something. I wish we would have been in a position to treat her as one of us, to find out her skills, to encourage her to work hard, and to teach her as much as we could. That is what I was doing with the 18-year-old kids we had brought with us. But instead her life went on as before: No cultural encounter took place.

Something for something should be the foundation of giving in all of our charities and welfare when working with people who can help themselves. It doesn't need to be fully reciprocal. The value of the something given doesn't have to equal the value of something received. The something given can be money or things, the something received an interaction of some kind. The something gained can be further education or training. It could be volunteering at charities, schools or churches. It can be helping kids with homework, reading to toddlers, cleaning up parks or helping elders, to name a few possibilities. For those working full time, this fact must be respected. But there are still simple things they could do that are valuable to the community; do not put a job at risk and help achieve a cultural encounter. The idea of something for something is to help us establish community, together, while the individual learns priceless life skills. The poor have much to offer our communities, and our communities have many needs.

The article "Our Miserable 21st Century"[57] lays out chilling statistics about the numbers of Americans who are living with alcohol abuse or drug addiction or are ex-cons. Many of these individuals live in poverty, and if we want to help them, we can't have government programs, charities and mentors ignore these challenges. Something for something can be our means to measure and address the problem. Here are three quotes from Eberstadt's article and comments as to why something for something could help us attack these problems. The point here is not that you agree with Eberstadt's statistics or his description of the attributes of the individuals, but that you recognize that something for something would be a positive policy step, even in these most difficult situations. Here is quote 1:

> We already knew from other sources (such as the U.S. Bureau of Labor Statistics "time use" surveys) that the overwhelming majority of the prime age men in this un-working army generally don't "do civil society" (charitable work, religious activities, volunteering), or for that matter much in the way of child care or help for others in the home either, despite abundance of time on their hands. Their routine, instead, typically centers on watching TV, DVDs, hand-held devices, etc., and roaming the Internet to the tune of an average of 2,000 hours a year. But Krueger's study adds a poignant and immensely sad detail to this portrait of daily life in 21st century America. In our mind's eye, we can now picture many millions of non-working men in the prime of life, out of work and not looking for jobs, sitting in front of TV screens — stoned.

Pulling these people back into our communities is paramount to helping them help themselves. Something for something will tell us whether they can contribute to society on a daily basis. If not, we need to address the reason why before we continue to pass along welfare benefits that enable the problem. Here is quote 2:

> Disability checks and means-tested benefits cannot support a lavish lifestyle. But they can offer a permanent alternative to paid employment, and for growing numbers of American men, they do. The rise of these programs has coincided with the death of work for larger and larger numbers of Americans not yet of retirement age. We cannot say that these programs *caused* the death of work for millions upon millions of younger men: What is incontrovertible, however, is that they have *financed* it.

Our communities have many needs, and lots of them don't require physical exertion, such as helping kids with homework or reading to toddlers. We can't let those on disability benefits check out of our communities. That is not good for them and not good for America. Something for something can pull them back in and should be a quid pro quo for receiving disability benefits from the government. Here is quote 3:

> We have to use rough estimates here rather than official numbers, because the government does not collect any data on the size or socioeconomic circumstances of this population of 20 million and never has. Amazing as this may sound and scandalous though it may be, America has, at least to date, effectively banished this huge group — a group roughly twice the total size of our illegal-immigrant population and an adult population larger than that of any state but California — to a near total and seemingly unending statistical invisibility. Our ex-cons are, so to speak, statistical outcasts who live in a darkness our polity does not care enough to illuminate — beyond the scope or interest of public policy, unless and until they next run afoul of the law.

Ex-convicts who are on welfare should contribute to our communities through something for something. If we are to be a positive force to help them turn their lives around, then we need to involve them in our communities. If they have no desire to contribute to our communities, then they shouldn't be entitled to benefits from welfare programs and charities.

POSTULATE 9

All charities and welfare programs should adopt something for something as the quid pro quo for the distribution of benefits. It should be established for each recipient with the idea of establishing community and pride. And it should be designed for the individual or family and constantly changed over time as needed.

We need something for something. When we give something, we need to get something. This means charity and welfare can't be a one-way street. This is an intellectual bomb to many working in the poverty sector. It goes against everything many religious leaders and poverty experts expound. Without it, we just have compassion, not effective compassion. Without it, it is too easy to ignore that which is most important — the human interaction to establish community. It is time for a quid pro quo for charity and a quid pro quo for welfare. Not a quid pro quo to establish punishment or judgment, but that establishes pride and community. The poor have much to offer. Let's use it.

In a 2016 national American Enterprise Institute (AEI) / Los Angeles Times survey, only 9% of respondents said that welfare benefits should be given to the poor with nothing received in return. Eighty-eight percent of respondents said they believed a better approach is to require poor people to seek work or job training if they are physically able to do so.[58] What was remarkable is that those in poverty had the same opinion.

The AEI Survey also polled people in poverty to understand how they felt about welfare. Only 13% believed poor people should be given benefits with nothing received in return. The poor want to contribute to the communities they live in. Americans need to know hand-outs must have something attached to them to translate to hand-ups. Something for something is the way to do that.

Something for something is the foundation to bring our poor back into the community. It is the final link to the three necessary postulates of change — discern the problems; get buy-in for improvement; and get something for something for benefits given out in the process. With those postulates we are ready to address poverty and make true strides toward fixing it. Far too many of us feel that addressing poverty is done as a moral obligation. But it's actually a great opportunity for self-fulfillment and pride. We like being teachers, managers, coaches and parents. We can be poverty busters too, with the same fulfillment of helping our fellow man. The next chapter will organize us for the journey.

12

SO WHAT DO WE DO NOW?

What you are being asked to consider is not a simple or an easy program.
But poverty is not a simple or an easy enemy. It cannot be driven from the
land by a single attack on a single front. Were this so we would have con-
quered poverty long ago. Nor can it be conquered by government alone.

— President Lyndon B. Johnson [59]

When did Americans outsource poverty? When did we subcontract poverty issues and concerns to government and a few charities? When did we stop being personally involved? When did Americans wash their hands of the problem?

> One hundred twenty-seven years ago, Americans directly waged war on poverty. In Baltimore, in 1891, The Association for Improving the Condition of the Poor (AICP) had 2,000 volunteers who made 8,227 visits to 4,025 families. Nearly half of those families were headed by widows, and they generally received material aid. Most of the others were headed by able-bodied men who generally received help in fighting alcohol and opium addiction and securing jobs. The personal involvement of rich and poor, not just material transfer, was evident in many ways. [60]

The description comes from *The Tragedy of American Compassion*, a book that walks through the history of Americans' interaction with the poor and their gradual disconnect over the last 127 years. Today if you ask Americans who is responsible for taking care of the poor, most would point to the government; 127 years ago, they would have said it was the citizens' job.

When President Lyndon Johnson declared the war on poverty in 1964, he said:

> This administration today, here and now, declares unconditional war on poverty in America. I urge this Congress and all Americans to join with me in that effort. It will not be a short or easy struggle, no single weapon or strategy will suffice, but we shall not rest until that war is won. The richest Nation on earth can afford to win it. We cannot afford to lose it. [61]

So the richest nation on earth got busy and the Great Society programs of the 1960s were launched. As the government stepped up to the war on poverty, the citizens stepped back. Perhaps that was unintended, but that is what happened. What is remembered today from the speech is the phrase "war on poverty." What isn't remembered is the phrase "all Americans to join me." Did that mean to support the government plan with taxes and votes or did it mean to get personally involved and work with the poor?

It is an interesting question, but a more relevant question is this: Is it possible for government to solve the poverty problem alone? I strongly believe the answer is no. It is a simple analysis that has been laid out in this book: To solve poverty we need discernment, mentoring and encouragement. Government alone can't do that effectively. To eradicate poverty, Americans have to show that they care about their fellow citizens by working with the poor and being a part of the community. Government can't do that, particularly the federal government, positioned far from communities throughout the states. Government can play an important role, but citizens are the secret to success.

Over the past 75 years, as government has stepped up, Americans have stepped back. We still care, we pay taxes and support charities, but most of us don't take personal responsibility for the poor. That is ironic, given the fact that Americans are some of the most charitable people on earth as described by President Kennedy:

> Few nations do more than the United States to assist their least fortunate citizens — to make certain that no child, no elderly or handicapped citizen, no family in any circumstances in any State, is left without the essential needs for a decent and healthy existence. In too few nations, I might add, are the people aware of the progressive strides this country has taken in demonstrating the humanitarian side of freedom. Our record is a proud one — and it sharply refutes those who accuse us of thinking only in the materialistic terms of cash registers and calculating machines. [62]

We are indeed a compassionate people, but compassion these days too often results in spending money and sometimes investing our time, but not in taking responsibility for the problem. It is time to reverse this trend. We need to focus on the problem of poverty as citizens motivated to fix it. Government must play an important role of financial support, and citizens must create a class encounter where we work with the poor directly. There is something in it for the conservative and for the progressive. Here are the arguments for both:

Based on government actions, it is especially easy for conservatives to wash their hands of poverty. We don't believe government should ever have been in the poverty business. It isn't provided in the Constitution as expressed by James Madison, who said, "I cannot undertake to lay my finger on that article of the Constitution which granted a right to Congress of expending, on objects of benevolence, the money of their constituents." [63]

It is easy to be cynical and think, "The government took on the war on poverty, it taxes me, I pay for it, so it should fix the problem." But overall poverty levels haven't dropped, welfare is very costly and the federal deficit is high and growing. We need to take the problem back and solve it. For every person who moves up the economic ladder to financial independence, the government programs are muted, and the deficit drops. Conservatives believe in less government and that their involvement as mentors with the poor can reduce government interference very effectively. I propose that it is not beneficial to argue whether the federal government should be in the poverty business. That ship has sailed. Instead, if conservatives did their part and personally worked at getting people out of poverty, everybody wins. Every person who no longer needs welfare grows the economy, makes our communities stronger and lowers the federal deficit.

I hope this argument works for conservatives, because we desperately need them to work the poverty problem. About half the nation's people are conservative or right-leaning. They are entrepreneurs, family folks, farmers, ranchers and hard workers. Most would be excellent mentors promoting independence, a work ethic and life skills. If we are ever going to make advances on the war on poverty, those on the right are going to have to pick up the fight. In fact, the fight will not be won without them.

Progressives

It is easy for progressives to trust in government to solve the poverty problem, because they believe that government is the people, and people can do this. We have faith in government and a proud history of building a safety net that has protected millions. But is the federal government the full solution to poverty? Can it be as effective as the community in having an impact on the personal lives of people? Aren't we putting too much pressure on government when we solely rely on it?

We want government to be successful; we want the war on poverty to be won; and we care about the downtrodden. Shouldn't we get involved and do our part? Aren't we helping the poor and the government when we do that? If we want the government to be successful, then we have to get involved personally.

I hope this argument works for progressives, because we desperately need them to personally work the poverty problem. About half the nation's people are progressive or left-leaning. They are teachers, blue collar workers, minorities and union members. Most would be excellent mentors on work ethic, education, community and life skills. If we are ever going to make advances on the war on poverty those on the left are going to have to pick up the fight. In fact, the fight will not be won without them.

Whether we are conservative, progressive or in-between, we need to get involved personally in the war on poverty. Government can, and should, be the money safety net, but people will have to be motivated to move up the economic ladder. I bet most presidents from FDR on through Kennedy, Johnson, Reagan and others would agree with that. I'm certain that if they saw how hard we tried to create a government solution, the programs we have created, and the money we've spent, they would most definitely agree. It is time we carved out the proper role for government, which is money support, and the proper role for citizens and charity — the personal touch.

POSTULATE
#10

POSTULATE 10

To win the war on poverty, Americans are going to have to stop relying on government alone.

Here is the plan each of us can follow if we want to win the war on poverty:

1. Vote and work to improve our welfare programs.

2. Volunteer our time to work directly with the poor.

3. Give our money and our time to effective charities.

These three points are covered in the next three chapters.

There is one other thing we need to do. We need to work to educate our fellow Americans about our plans and beliefs so that we can reach critical mass. When that is accomplished, we will make progress in the war on poverty.

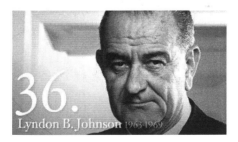

It has been quite a journey since President Johnson declared war on poverty. Over 50 years we have created numerous government welfare programs to fight that war. Step one of the new war on poverty is to adjust federal welfare to provide a safety net that works while providing the impetus for individuals to move up the economic ladder of success. We can do this. But we need to start by looking behind the curtain of the federal welfare programs, categorize them and then get our hands around them. All in one chapter. It can be done, and we will do it.

13

GOVERNMENT PROGRAMS AND WELFARE

The negative income tax would be a satisfactory reform of our present welfare system only if it replaces the host of other specific programs that we now have. It would do more harm than good if it simply became another rag in the ragbag of welfare programs.

— *Milton Friedman* [64]

For an accountant the federal budget is the holy grail of budgets. It is the big budget with all the zeros. One day in 1993 while working as a chief financial officer for a small oil and gas company, I was walking by the federal building in downtown Denver and I looked inside. There it was, the federal budget in a large loose=leaf book. I couldn't help myself. I bought it and thus started an unusual accounting hobby of tracking federal spending and trying to understand our government through numbers.

Later I also bought the statistical abstract of the United States — a marvelous book of all kinds of wonderful statistics on people, income, jobs and poverty. My accounting hobby had now strayed into economics. One night while looking through the budget, I wondered what we spent each year on welfare. It sounded simple enough. I'd merely find the department of welfare and see what it spent. But it doesn't work that way. Welfare is spread throughout the budget in several agencies. The problem is that the agencies do other things too, so that finding welfare meant searching, parsing agency budgets and adding it up.

I concluded that welfare cost us $170 billion. My statistical abstract book said that there were 35.7 million people in poverty. It also told me how much additional income they needed to be out of poverty. I did the math and found we needed $85 billion to pull every American out of poverty. I was dumbfounded. How can that be? According to my numbers, we spent more than twice the amount needed to solve poverty and yet we had all these people in poverty. I checked my math, studied more, but the relationship was true. I had no idea what to do with my newfound discovery. I simply went back to work. The late-night revelation sat on the shelf for 23 years.

It took an early, partial retirement in 2010 before I had the luxury to address my revelation. By then everything was on the Internet. "This will be easy," I thought. Still, it took me weeks of study to ascertain whether the relationship was still true. It was. "All those years have passed," I thought, "and yet in so many ways not much has changed." I started to ponder why that was and what it meant to both users and taxpayers. But overriding that question was a feeling of frustration and annoyance that understanding the American welfare system is too complicated and mysterious. I felt Americans deserve better.

Over time, I became committed to trying to educate people about the makeup and function of our welfare system. I created a website called FederalSafetyNet. com and published my findings. No fees, no advertising, just information culled from the vast array of reports, budgets, books and experts.

Four years later it was one of the top listings in a Google search of U.S. Welfare, Safety Net, welfare issues, welfare fraud and other welfare and poverty topics. It beat the government sites and think tanks with large budgets and armies of researchers. It does so because people were hungry for simple and summarized information across all programs.

So here is our federal welfare system simplified. By my count there are 13 welfare programs in America as follows:

Negative Income Tax. Two tax credit programs are administered by the Internal Revenue Service (IRS) to distribute money to low-income Americans. The two programs are the Earned Income Tax Credit (EITC), and the Child Tax Credit (CTC). The tax credits include a refundable portion which is paid to individuals and families who owe no income tax for the year. Therefore, this portion of the tax credits acts as negative income tax.

SNAP (Supplemental Nutrition Assistance Program). This is a food program for low-income individuals and families. SNAP used to be called the food stamp program. It is run by the USDA (United States Department of Agriculture). Participants receive a debit card that is accepted in most grocery stores for the purchase of food.

Housing Assistance. Various housing programs are administered by the Department of Housing and Urban Development (HUD), including rental assistance, public housing and various community development grants.

SSI (Supplemental Security Income). Administered by the Social Security Administration, this program pays cash to low-income individuals over 65 or under 65 if blind or disabled.

Pell Grants. This is a grant program administered by the Department of Education to distribute up to $5,935 to students from low-income households to promote postsecondary education (colleges and trade schools).

TANF (Temporary Assistance for Needy Families). Administered by HHS (the U.S. Department of Health and Human Services), this is a combined federal and state program that pays cash to low-income households with the goal of moving people from welfare to work.

Child Nutrition. These are food programs administered by the USDA that include school lunch, breakfast and after-school programs. They target children from low-income households and provide free or reduced priced meals.

Head Start. Administered by HHS, this is a preschool program available to kids from low-income families.

Job Training Programs. These are many training programs administered by the Department of Labor (DOL) to provide job training, displacement and employment services that target low-income Americans.

WIC (Women, Infants and Children). Administered by the USDA and available to low-income households, WIC provides food to pregnant women and children up to five years of age.

Child Care. (Administered by HHS) is a block grant program available to states and local public and private agencies that administer child care programs to low-income families.

LIHEAP (Low Income Home Energy Assistance Program). Administered by HHS, the program aids low-income households that pay a high proportion of household income for home energy (heating or cooling).

Lifeline (Obama Phone). Administered by the FCC (Federal Communications Commission), the program provides discounted phone service, including cell phones and broadband Internet service, to low-income individuals.

All of the programs listed above are means-tested, meaning that to qualify individuals and families must have an annual income below a certain level. Because they are all aimed at helping low-income people, I have included them with welfare programs. The diverse and independent programs have complex rules for qualification and use.

In total the programs spent $354.5 billion in 2017[65]. There are two observations that summarize the welfare system. The first is the Poverty Gap, which demonstrates that we spend twice as much money on welfare programs than it takes to move every person in the U.S. out of poverty. The second is the historic poverty level. Even though we have dramatically increased spending on welfare programs over the last 50 years, the poverty level has not dropped. These facts are demonstrated below.

Poverty Gap

In 2017 there were 12.6 million single people and 7.8 million families in a poverty status in America. In all we spent $355 billion on welfare in 2017. Census Bureau numbers tell us those in poverty are collectively $178 billion shy of the poverty threshold. Therefore we spent twice what it would cost to end poverty in America.[66] This is a powerful fact that tells us how much money we have to work with to wipe out poverty in our nation. A resource restructured as cash payments to the poor structured in a way that promotes work would be a powerful tool to fight poverty.

Poverty and spending over the years

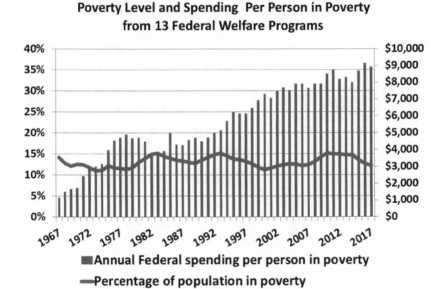

The chart above shows the percentage of the population in poverty and welfare spending per person in poverty over the last 50 years. It is not a pretty picture. The line is the percentage of the population in poverty in the U.S. has remained flat for 50 years ranging, between about 12% to 15% of the population. The bars are the spending per person in poverty, which is the sum of the cost of the 13 programs listed above divided by the number of people in poverty. It shows that we spent less than $1,159 per person in poverty in 1967 compared to $8,930 per person in 2017.[67]

We have spent more and more, but the poverty percentage hasn't dropped much. We have made lives more comfortable, but we have not moved people to financial independence. Many people have used the system as a safety net to achieve financial independence, while others have been in the system for years, some decades.

No discernment, buy-in, or something for something

There is much debate as to why the poverty level has been so stubborn. But perhaps the easiest way to understand why is to see that the welfare system is missing the key ingredients for success — discernment, buy-in and something for something. The system is not designed as a hand-up. The benefits are generally just hand-outs with nothing expected in return. The whole system is uncoordinated, and the collective benefits are not graduated to income, meaning that people can lose more in benefits then they gain from work. The same is true for marriage. Marriage often results in overall lost benefits to the individuals when the entire system is considered.[68]

Public opinion on welfare

We could spend a long time analyzing our complex and bifurcated system to attempt to prove that it is ineffective, or we could rely on public opinion, which says it all. In 2016 the American Enterprise Institute along with the *Los Angeles Times* conducted a survey of 1,202 adults whereby 235 were in poverty at the time of the survey.[69] Here is what the poor think of our welfare system:

- - 55% believe that the main purpose behind welfare is to help poor people get back on their feet again. 39% believe it is to provide for the needs of poor people while they are poor, and the balance had no opinion.

- - 40% believe that government efforts to fight poverty have made things worse for the poor, and 12% believe the government efforts have had no impact. 34% believe government efforts have had some impact and only 8% believe government has had a big impact.

- - 42% believe that when poverty programs failed, it was primarily because they were not well-designed. 23% believe it was because the benefits did not get to the poor, and only 29% believe it was because not enough money was spent to make a difference.

So the majority of the poor in our nation believe we should teach a man to fish instead of just giving him fish. And that our government programs have failed in this regard and that the programs are poorly designed and don't get enough of the benefits to the poor. That pretty much says it all, and it comes from the users of the system. That is a powerful commentary.

Changes to our welfare system

Welfare needs some basic changes if it is going to work in concert with individuals to reduce poverty. Here is what we should do:

1. The system has to be simplified to pay cash to individuals instead of in-kind benefits such as housing, food or preschool.

2. The formula for qualification and distribution of cash has to be established to encourage work, not penalize marriage and increased financial independence.

3. A quid pro quo must be established to get something for something for the welfare paid out.

The goal of government should be to establish a money floor for individuals, and to do so in a way that does not discourage work. This means that for every dollar from work the individuals earn, they would lose only a portion of their welfare benefit — say 50 cents, so they always come out ahead.

In the words of Friedman:

> The negative income tax would have enormous advantages. It is directed specifically at the problem of poverty. It gives help in the form most useful to the recipient, namely, cash. It is general — it does not give help because the recipient is old or disabled or sick or lives in a particular area, or any of the other many specific features entitling people to benefits under current programs. It gives help because the recipient has a low income. It makes explicit the cost borne by taxpayers. Like any other measure to alleviate poverty, it reduces the incentive of people who are helped to help themselves. However, if the subsidy rate is kept at a reasonable level, it does not eliminate that incentive entirely. An extra dollar earned always means more money available for spending.[70]

Such a negative income tax or guaranteed income program is indeed possible and easy to structure. Such a program has been laid out in the website FederalSafetyNet.com.[71] It establishes a starting point of $8,000 per adult and $5,000 per child in poverty. It reduces the payments by 50 cents per $1.00 earned from individuals and 10 cents reduction in the child payment per $1.00 earned by the parent. If adults are living in a single household, then the second adult gets

$3,500 as a guaranteed income, because he or she can share household expenses such as rent.

The program would have cost under $255 billion in fiscal year 2017. In that same year, we spent $355 billion on the 13 federal programs. This allowed us to adopt a guaranteed payment and still save $100 billion annually on the federal deficit. This is a sad commentary on the inefficiency and high cost of our current bifurcated welfare system. That is the bad news; the good news is that if we fix it, we can get more cash available to the poor and save billions toward the federal deficit.

Something for something

Perhaps the biggest problem of our current welfare programs is that they do not require something for something. If we made one change to welfare that would be it. It could include contributing time to any community needs such as volunteer work in day-care centers, schools, nursing homes or charities. It could be modeled after community service that many courts use today.

The something gained doesn't have to be of equal worth to the benefits given, but it has to be something. It can start small and build over time. If a person is working full time, that would be factored into the obligation. If a person is enrolled in a training program or obtaining a degree, that also would be factored in. The goal is to involve the poor within the community. We have many needs in our communities, such as cheaper child care. Having those on welfare help our communities can accomplish many things, such as:

1. Communities get help where they need it.

2. We tell the poor they are important and matter to the community.

3. We develop life skills.

4. We stop cheaters.

5. We combat idleness.

Here is what John F. Kennedy said when addressing welfare in a speech to Congress:

> We must find ways of returning far more of our dependent people to independence. We must find ways of returning them to a participating and productive role in the community. One sure way is by providing the opportunity every American cherishes to do sound and useful work. For this reason, I am recommending a change in the law to permit States to maintain with Federal financial help community work and training projects for unemployed people

receiving welfare payments. Under such a program, unemployed people on welfare would be helped to retain their work skills or learn new ones; and the local community would obtain additional manpower on public projects.

But earning one's welfare payment through required participation in a community work or training project must be an opportunity for the individual on welfare, not a penalty. Federal financial participation will be conditioned upon proof that the work will serve a useful community or public purpose, will not displace regular employees, will not impair prevailing wages and working conditions, and will be accompanied by certain basic health and safety protections. Provisions must also be made to assure appropriate arrangements for the care and protection of children during the absence from home of any parent performing work or undergoing training. [72]

President Kennedy laid out good ground rules for something for something. He knew that to truly help the poor, we needed to help get them back to meaningful roles within our communities. He was right.

Introducing something for something within our welfare programs would require much of the work to be done by local charities and even businesses to work directly with the poor. Washington can pay the benefits to the poor, but local communities, local government, charities and businesses need to work with the poor directly and establish the something we get back.

Minimum wage and higher-paying jobs

Good-paying jobs and lots of them are a key ingredient in the poverty fight. The government must do all it can to support the private sector to create good jobs and promote higher wages. As shown in chapter five, 96 million Americans, almost a third of the populace, live in households with income below the level of a living wage (two times the poverty threshold). The website TalkPoverty.org said the market is failing to provide enough jobs. The jobs that are available are often inadequate because they do not offer enough hours, and schedules are volatile, which makes it difficult to supplement with additional income."

While jobs are important, poverty is stubborn even in times of low unemployment such as we had in 2017. The poverty rate was 12.3% for the year, even though the unemployment rate was under 5%. The reason for this is not a lack of good-paying jobs, but other life circumstances preventing those in poverty from working. Sixty-three percent of working-age adults in poverty (18–64 years of age) did not work in the year, and another 13% spent at least part of the year out of the workforce. The reason given for being absent from the workforce included illness, disability, school, home and family reasons. "Could not find a job" accounted for only 6% of why those in poverty were not participants in the workforce. [73]

Minimum-wage laws are popular today as a means of getting wages up. However, such laws make entry level jobs more difficult to justify, and these jobs are crucial in gaining life skills. Nobody can gain a work ethic without learning how to work, and to do so we all need to start at the bottom and work our way up. We need more employers willing to hire a 16-year-old at $5.00 an hour for a couple hours to sweep out the shop and in the meantime to work with the youth. The more requirements we put on employers the less employment we will have.

The solution to higher wages is to attach it at the federal level with a guaranteed income. That really becomes a wage subsidy that is fair and targets what we want — higher income to those in need. Forcing employers to achieve our welfare goals hasn't worked well in the past and won't in the future.

Can federal welfare programs be changed?

What should be done with welfare is a very contentious issue in the U.S. About half the country believes the system should be expanded to more people and cover more needs. The other half thinks we spend way too much, and the system should be shrunk or even eliminated. Half the country believes welfare is an essential system to protect the poor from the ravages of free enterprise, and the other half believes the system encourages poverty and traps people into lives of dependency. Arguing this point has resulted in a stalemate. So nothing consequential has been done regarding welfare for decades. The only way out of this impasse is to make changes that work for both sides.

POSTULATE
#11

POSTULATE 11

Fix federal welfare by rolling up the current programs to give benefits as cash and structure payments so they encourage work, marriage and financial independence, and get something for something for the benefits distributed.

This change to federal welfare is the only change that seems capable of getting majority support. Progressives will like getting more cash to the poor, and conservatives will like getting something for something.

Without meaningful change to the federal welfare system, it will be hard to make progress moving people out of poverty. Still, citizen involvement can do much to offset the lack of motivation built into the welfare system. Most poor people do not want to be dependent on government. Citizens should attempt to rescue the situation by their involvement. A life moved from dependence to independence is an amazing achievement. It would be great if the government fixed welfare by substituting a cash floor under its citizens to encourage self-independence. But perhaps we could render the need for such a system settled if citizens get involved and solve the poverty problem themselves. We are closer to that solution than we think. It can be done. It just takes work by all of us to solve a piece of the problem. If each of us mentored one person in poverty, we could solve the problem. Based upon the population of the U.S., all it would take is one out of every four people to work with one person in poverty. That's very doable.

14

MENTOR

If it be true that the children of the poor today are themselves destined to be the impoverished parents of tomorrow, then some social intervention is needed to break the cycle, to interrupt the circuits of hunger and hopelessness that link generation to generation.

— *Mollie Orshansky* [74]

In 1963 Orshansky was right when she said that a social intervention was going to be necessary to stop the cycle of poverty. What we know now a half-century later is that social intervention can't solely come from government. Therefore it falls to the people. It is our job. We have to take responsibility back. That will be difficult for a people who have become comfortable with reliance on government. To fix the problem of poverty will take a personal hand-up.

Mother Teresa

Perhaps Mother Teresa can help us. To work with those in poverty, she ultimately took a personal vow of poverty and devoted her life to the poor. That is remarkable, but it isn't realistic for most of us. Still, she has the secret. She said:

"Poverty is freedom. It is a freedom so that what I possess doesn't own me, so that what I possess doesn't hold me down, so that my possessions don't keep me from sharing or giving of myself."[75] Those last words are the haunting ones: Too many possessions keep us from giving of ourselves. So let's not do that. Let's give of ourselves. That means investing our emotions and our time to help those less fortunate than us. Simple as that. We can do that. In fact, most Americans have an inner voice pushing them toward helping others. We are the most giving society on earth. We just need to channel that giving.

Each of us needs to take one life to mentor, one family to help. This is not a call to get rid of our possessions, change our jobs, scale down our living expenses or change our lives. It is a call to make room in our lives to help someone solve the poverty problem. It means making ourselves available to help people obtain their financial independence.

We need to adopt Mother Teresa's attitude on giving. Most of us know that helping another person is one of the most rewarding endeavors in life. We live it every day as parents, teachers, coaches, supervisors and workers. But we have to give of our time in an effective manner. We have to help about 40 million Americans get out of poverty. We have to do it as individuals — one-on-one. There are more than 200 million adults in America who are not in poverty. If just one-fourth of us took one person and helped that individual, we could make a big difference in helping eliminate poverty. Each case will be unique; each person will require individual mentoring. We have to adopt the principles in this book and get to work.

Mother Teresa also said: "We have no right to judge the rich. For our part, what we desire is not a class struggle but a class encounter, in which the rich save the poor, and the poor save the rich."[76]

That is the secret we have forgotten. That the rich can help the poor and the poor can help the rich. If we believe that to be true, we will solve the poverty problem in America. If we believe that to be untrue we are destined to have distinct social classes in America that operate independently of one another. If you aren't sure whether it is true or not, find a person outside your social class and interface with him. Good things happen to our souls when we interact with one another. That doesn't mean that it is easy. Far from it. It will be frustrating and time-consuming, but in the end, our souls will be strengthened, and that makes it all worthwhile.

We do indeed need a class encounter. We need an interface between those in poverty and the middle and upper class. The poor must realize that they can climb out of poverty if they work hard and meet those trying to help them halfway. They can't just expect a handout.

Mother Teresa also said: "We know what that poverty means, first of all, to be hungry for bread, to need clothing and to not have a home. But there is a far greater kind of poverty. It means being unwanted, unloved and neglected. It means having no one to call your own." [77] Our welfare programs try to address "bread, clothing and home" but they don't address "unwanted, unloved and neglected." For that we need caring individuals. That is why when we look for government to be the solution to poverty, we come up short.

That takes us to the last postulate, Postulate 12: To solve poverty, people are going to have to get involved personally as mentors and friends of the poor. Mentors are going to have to encourage education, hard work, basic life skills and good decisions. Mentors are going to have to show that they care and want to help the poor to integrate into the community and contribute to the community.

A hundred years ago in America, the word compassion was used most often in its literal meaning: "to suffer with." [78] Today our definition is "sympathetic consciousness of others' distress together with a desire to alleviate it." [79] Desire is no longer enough; we have to have action. We have to "suffer with" if together we hope to solve poverty. We can focus government on what it does best, and people at what they do best. Government can provide a floor of economic stability, and then people are going to have to pick up the fight from there. We shouldn't expect quick fixes or magic formulas. We should work together on life's challenges to make progress that we individually define. Interface one-on-one. Employ the postulates in this book, find a person or family and get started. Work together consistently and persistently. Take a great adventure together — and best of luck. You are both worth it.

15

CHARITIES

"We hold that the chief need of the poor to-day is not alms giving, but the moral support of true friendship."

— *A Handbook of Charity Organization* [80]

It isn't money that is missing from the fight on poverty. It is time. Time from people willing to mentor and time from those in poverty willing to learn. We are all a product of being helped to become self-sufficient. The guidance usually comes from loving parents and family. Many people become self-sufficient without that help, but the route is harder. But no one makes it without support, instruction, advice and mentors along the way. There is so much to learn about money, spending, budgeting, saving, debt avoidance, hard work, attitude, personal hygiene, interviewing, job skills, career paths, personal interests and skills, education, study skills, testing skills, government programs, child-rearing and child education, to name a few examples.

Mentoring is important, but equally important is encouragement, interaction and involving the poor in community. In sum, friendship. People need to hear that they are important and matter, that their efforts are appreciated, that we know what they are up against, and that we are pulling for their success. This isn't just lip service. The poor represent one of the keys to our nation's success. Those in poverty represented 12.3% of the population in 2017. We can't financially write off 12.3% of the population and have the economy and communities we desire.

I wish most people had the ability to work directly with the poor and mentor them. But the fact is that many of the middle class and wealthy in our nation simply don't interface with the poor and are not sure how to solve the problem. The simple answer is to respond when you face an encounter. As we interact with the poor in our everyday lives, we need to be cognizant of needs we could help address. That doesn't mean a lecture or condescension, but rather interactive learning and caring. We need to find the time to start with a simple conversation and then follow up as a friend and mentor.

Many people in America do this on a daily basis, but as a society we need a more direct path to organize such a class encounter. We need a formal means of getting the middle class and wealthy in our nation to interact with the poor. That linkage can be supplied by charities. Charities can be the interface between the poor and those who want to be friends and mentors.

However, to do that we are going to need a different kind of charity. We are going to need charities that work with the poor and have volunteers willing to give their time in order to make a difference. It is not enough for a charity to merely hand out benefits like food or clothing. It also needs to organize a class interaction to establish community.

I'm lucky enough to be involved in such a charity in Parker Colorado — the Parker Task Force. It started as a food bank but is now so much more. It's a food bank that changes lives. It took over 20 years to mature and get the community behind it. As it developed, it steadily gravitated toward wanting to make people self-sufficient as much as it wanted to cure hunger and destitution. It pulled in local citizens willing to donate half a day a week to work with the poor as counselors. It developed great policies on how to interview clients, how to keep data confidential and how to work together with the poor to come up with a plan for self-sufficiency. It limited clients to just 10 visits to obtain food or other benefits, which established a sense of urgency to make progress. Here is how they did it:

Discern. The food bank interviews everyone who comes through the door to learn about their lives and to work on an individualized plan to become self-sufficient.

Buy-in. The food bank turns away anyone that does not agree with the idea he/she would work together to change lives. Such a client might get a visit or two to stabilize the family with food and rent, but if the plan wasn't developed, the aid stopped.

Something for something. Together the counselors and the clients established practical steps toward accomplishing financial independence. That could start with changing careers, cutting expenses, finding new living arrangements, getting the kids in school or addressing a health problem, for example. If the plan wasn't followed, more people got involved to offer ideas, encouragement and follow-up. If the client stops making progress or really isn't interested in becoming self-sufficient, the aid stops, and the relationship is put on hold. Fortunately, this happens only occasionally. We are thankful that most clients get their lives back. And all this usually happens in under 10 visits to the food bank.

About the Parker Task Force (PTF)

The PTF is an all-volunteer organization. This helps keep the perspective of the organization's goals. It is citizen helping citizen, and there are no politics concerning hitting targets for fund-raising or justifying their existence by addressing a need. The operation is set up so that it helps citizens in need in any way that promotes solutions, such as rent payments, child care, food, personal hygiene and job search.

We are fortunate to have the PTF. The community sends those in need to the Task Force for help and organizes volunteers to mentor them. The *Handbook of Charity Organization* describes a charity in Buffalo, New York, to mentor the poor. Much of the book lays out basic recommendations for how to set up and establish such a charity. I was struck by one observation from the book:

> Besides, in the suppression of some of the grosser evils which we have mentioned, not even the first step in reform can be taken except by the co-operation of all classes, all creeds, all parties in the community; unless all band together for the attainment of a common objective. So firmly rooted have the abuses become, that nothing short of the bandied strength of the whole community can ever suppress them. [81]

It is true that the whole community needs to get involved in a coordinated effort to work on poverty. The PTF has a relationship with the town, the schools and the churches, all of which try to coordinate their efforts. The police in Parker carry vouchers from PFT for a paid night in a hotel if they find someone they feel should be taken off the streets. The next day they are encouraged to visit the Task Force and be interviewed.

One other observation in the book was startling. It went through a whole section on how to mentor the poor. Guess the No. 1 rule. It described the mentor as a "volunteer visitor," and here is the No. 1 rule: In accordance with the fundamental principles of the plan, "the visitor is required strictly to abstain from giving relief or being the almoner of the charity of others." [82]

In other words, the No. 1 rule on mentoring is give no money. Can you imagine that? A charity recommending that people work with the poor but spend no money in the endeavor. I know why they recommend that, and it makes perfect sense. To be good mentors to the poor, it is counterproductive to also be the supplier of money, food or benefits. Instead, it is important for them to give of their time. They need to give the alms of good advice not the alms themselves. Those alms can come from government, charity, family or friends, but not the mentor.

It works this way at PTF also. The counselor is the mentor, the friend working with the client. The counselors give no money or benefits but help the clients maneuver through the benefits they can receive from the charity and other sources of aid, such as government programs. The counselor becomes a friend and confident of the person, and they work together to solve problems.

If all goes well, they can achieve what is described in the *Handbook of Charity Organization*:

> The Buffalo Society to-day has the confidence of the entire community, and even the poor now see that we are their true friends; so much so, that our Agents are often stopped as they are on their way to investigate cases, with the request, "Do just stop in, and see how nicely I'm getting along." [83]

Across America there are many people who would experience this same interaction when meeting someone they once helped. In affluent communities like Parker, goals are easier to achieve compared with the inner cities where mental illness, drugs, crime, missing parents and poor schools have dug a deep hole. Those that work in such situations deserve our attention, praise and help. While the route to financial independence is harder in these places, the steps are the same. We need to discern the problems, make plans to solve them and get busy. The biggest missing ingredient is time — time for successful people to reach out and get involved. Once we hit critical mass with enough people paying attention, we can change lives.

The middle class in our nation has had a pass worrying about the poor. We relegated that responsibility to government long ago. We reason that if we pay our taxes, it is up to government to solve the poverty problem. That pass is up. We have done that for over 50 years, and poverty is as high now as when we started. Government will never be able to solve the poverty problem alone. It was never intended to be the sole solution, but somehow it is perceived as so. No more.

People have to get involved. We must all do our part. When enough of us spend time working with the poor, we will see progress on a national scale.

Fixing our federal poverty programs would help, but so would fixing many of our charities. Too many exist as hand-outs with no attempt to get to know and influence those they serve. In his book *Toxic Charity*, Robert D. Lupton's proposes an "Oath of Compassionate Service" that charities and mentors should follow:

Never do for the poor what they can do for themselves.

- Limit one-way giving to emergency situations.

- Strive to empower the poor through employment, lending and invest-ing, using grants sparingly to reinforce achievements.

- Subordinate self-interests to the needs of those being served.

- Listen closely to those you seek to help, especially to what is not being said. Unspoken feelings may contain essential clues to effective service.

- Above all, do no harm. [84]

Lupton goes on to describe a new kind of charity aimed at boosting up the poor.

> What if we asked ourselves, "What outcomes would we actu-ally like to see from our charity?" And then began to restructure our giving to produce those very results. If we cared about, for instance, seeing human dignity enhanced, or trusting relationships being formed, or self-sufficiency increasing, then we could employ proven methods known to accomplish these goals. We know that trust grows with accountability over time. We know that mutual exchange and legitimate negotiating is energizing (people of every culture love to bargain!). And we know that employment starts people on the path to self-reliance. We know these things. And we have the capacity to accomplish them. But the will to change our traditional charity systems — now that is the real challenge. [85]

Americans support thousands of charities working with the poor across our nation. Before we send them money, we should make sure they are truly effective. Along with Lupton's oath, here are some questions we could ask ourselves before we support a charity with our donations and time.

1. Does the charity distinguish between those individuals who can help them-selves versus those who cannot?

2. Does the charity measure its success by the benefits it pays out or by the lives it changes?

3. Does the charity discern, obtain buy-in and get something for something?

30 million–word gap

There is one more item that charities must address. It is the 30 million–word gap. That comes from an amazing book titled *The Social World of Children Learning to Talk* by Betty Hart and Todd R. Risley. Here is what they did and what they learned:

> Each month for 2½ years, we recorded in their homes the interactions between 42 children and their parents as the children learned to talk. We spent 10 more years creating and verifying an immense computer database in order both to preserve the priceless gift of these families' willingness to be watched and to ensure that the database would be one of a kind in the depth and scientific integrity of its information about the everyday experience of young American children.[86]

Further, they write:

> The 42 families that we observed included 13 families in professional and managerial occupations, 23 working-class families and six families living on welfare. Of the children, 23 were girls, 17 were African American, and one was Hispanic.[87]

> When we grouped families by SES [Socioeconomic Status], we discovered that the most important differences among families was not the relative advantages conferred by education or income but the amount of talking the parents did with their children.[88]

> At age 3 … the children of the talkative group had accumulated 46 million words of language experience, 17 million more than the average child and 31 million more than children of the taciturn group.[89]

Hart and Risley add:

> The data of the children in the taciturn group remind us that in some American cultures conversation between adults and children is considered pointless or inappropriate.[90]

> But, the data showed that no matter what the family SES, the more time parents spent talking with their child from day to day, the more rapidly the child's vocabulary was likely to be growing and the higher the child's score on an IQ test was likely to be at age 3.[91]

These differences in the amount of early family experience translate into striking disparities in the children's accomplishments at age 3 in terms of predictors of success in school and the workplace, such as IQ scores, vocabulary growth rates and vocabulary use.[92]

If we wanted to do one thing today to help kids stay out of poverty it would be to make sure every child gets 46 million words by the time the child is three years old. That means conversation, not TV or media. All of us can talk to kids, whether old or young, healthy or disabled, rich or poor. Does this speak to you? If so, get involved. We need some new charities to get us organized and help parents understand the importance of talking to their children. We can also do some of the talking ourselves and supply some of the 46 million words. What a great way to bust poverty.

Local saints

Nancy Gripman teaching a young child to read

It is with the fondest memory I think back on Nancy Gripman, who was one of the founders of the Parker Task Force. Nancy died in 2015. She was 86 years old and had done so much in our community that she died nothing short of sainthood. No national acclaim, not even statewide notoriety. But in the little hamlet we live in, she touched many lives. So much so that the town erected a statue of her in a park.

Nancy isn't alone. Many people do great work and give of their time and treasure. Most probably don't get to see the long-term results of their efforts or even get so much as a thank-you. But their work is important, and they are changing lives. I, at least, can say thank you. Thank you from a grateful nation.

16

A GREAT BIG UNWAVERING HEART

In colonial America, emphasis on a theistic God of both justice and mercy led to an understanding of compassion that was hard-headed but warm-hearted.

— Marvin Olasky, *The Tragedy of American Compassion* [93]

Thanks to her, 4,425 kids in poverty received Christmas gifts this year. Not just any gift, but a new toy moms and dads got to pick for their children. Jessica Bachus runs Kenzi's Causes, a charity in Denver that among other things sponsors a toy store each year in early December that allows parents in poverty to pick out a toy for their child — a brand-new toy that the parent knows the child wants. Over a thousand parents and guardians come through the store in one day. She needed help managing the line outside the door. I volunteered gladly. While I was happy to help, I must confess I also had an ulterior motive. I wanted to see how such a system would work. I wanted to understand how she could possibly get that many toys in the hands of that many people who were truly needy. But I was also a sucker for her enthusiasm and drive. It was contagious. I wanted to see Bachus in action.

Jessica Bachus working the toy store in Denver, Colorado

So there I was in the freezing cold one December day putting numbered bracelets on the wrists of a thousand people in line. It was like those wristbands they put on you in the hospital — once on you can't take it off and still use it. The bracelet gave the people in line a number and organized who got in the store when. She figured that if it was important enough for people to wait in line for hours in the cold, it meant they needed help. Some waited all night in below-zero temperatures. Most waited several hours. I told Bachus I would work the line because I wanted to meet the people. I wanted to get an assessment of who was getting free toys and whether the family was really in need. I came away thinking she had a pretty good formula.

Throughout it all, there was Bachus back and forth, coordinating volunteers, policing the proceedings and moving things along. What a heart — a great big wonderful heart. But it wasn't just that; it was her energy and skill that also amazed me. She worked all year long for this one day. She did fundraising events, bought toys on discount, coordinated toy drives and sought free stuff from manufacturers. All that to get toys in the hands of kids she never met.

She had one rule for the participants — they had to have an ID and a copy of the birth certificate of their child. That was how she policed what toys parents were allowed to take. She kept it simple, and her compassion flowed. But during my work in the line, I saw another side of Bachus. A young mother said she didn't have the birth certificates because they had been lost in an apartment fire. I called Bachus over so she could hear the story directly from the mom, who was in tears. The story unfolded, and Bachus listened. She never wavered an inch. No certificates, no toys. I was a bit taken aback. No exceptions, period. Bachus had the biggest of hearts but the toughest of minds.

I went on to work the line that day following Bachus's recommendation that I always put the bracelets on the people myself. I made some exceptions to that procedure, and they came back to haunt me. One father explained to me he had to go to work later, and he needed a bracelet for his wife, who was on the way. I gave him one. Fifteen minutes later, two people came up asking for bracelets using the man as an example. I heard about how it was a fabricated story and he had given the bracelet to someone who had not waited in line and was not his wife. In another instance, a sweet-looking young girl explained that her mom was in the bathroom and that if I would give her the bracelet, she would give it to her mom. I told her to go get her mom and I'd put the bracelet on when she found me. Over an hour later and two new stories, there was still no mom. There were line jumpers I had to send to the back; there were people with wild stories of how I missed them, and they should get to go ahead, and about every hard-luck story you could imagine. I got the Bachus point quickly. Without good process and standards, things fall apart.

Setting up the Kenzi's Causes Toy Store in Denverb

Bachus has the right combination. A big heart and an unwavering commitment to a process she believes is fair and effective. She wants the parents to be Santa Claus. Otherwise it wounds pride. Bachus's big heart is unwavering. She understands that "no good deed goes unpunished." But such negative events don't slow her down. I thought about that during frustrating moments as I was working the line. More than once I wanted to shout, "Why are you lying to me?" or "Can't everyone just get along?" or "I'm freezing, and I don't need this." But then I'd see a mom and dad with a big smile loading a sack of toys in an old car trunk or Bachus hugging a tired child volunteer or a single mom hoping the right toy was still there for her three-year-old.

This is the attitude we must all adopt. Big hearts and tough love. The debate shouldn't be that we need tough love. The debate should be about where the boundaries are. What expectations are unyielding? What is the definition of meeting halfway? What defines a hand up not a hand out? What is the unwavering part of our great big hearts? It is the same question we struggle with as parents, teachers, coaches or managers. Such care and love need to be brought to the fight against poverty. Lupton sums it up well in his book *Toxic Charity*.

> If there is one take away message that this book can offer to those in service work or supporting it, it is this: the poor, no matter how destitute, have enormous untapped capacity; find it, be inspired by it, and build upon it. [94]

We must never give up on those in poverty. We will hope and pray that those of able mind and sound body can gain their financial independence and lead the lives they desire. We will work as mentors and give of our time and money. But we must be unwavering in our expectations and our approach. Because it isn't about us; it is about them, and we want them to succeed. We want to build community together with both of us contributing. When we need inspiration, we ought to think of Jessica Bachus, FDR, Mollie Orshansky, Pastor Susan Lyon, Bob Cote, Benjamin Franklin, Robert Lupton and the countless people out there working the problem every day. Give us strength to have a great big but unwavering heart.

ACKNOWLEDGEMENTS

Thousands of people are fighting the war on poverty in America, and I have been fortunate to work alongside a few of the best of you. Your grace and wisdom wore off on me, and I am forever grateful. Special thanks to:

Steve Budnack, Volunteer Chairman of the Parker Task Force. We consider ourselves fortunate to have you in our community. You are the rare leader who knows how to get things done in a complex organization. Most important, you know how to raise money to ensure its success and yet have that special mojo to work one-on-one with the poor and make a difference. And you do it all without taking a dime for your labor. Truly an inspiration to all of us. And you were gracious enough to take me along for part of the ride.

Eric and Linda Szaloczi, Mike Batzer and Richelle Pfeiffer, fellow founders of the Blue Mountain Foundation. We have struggled together for 13 years, trying to give our money to the right organizations that will make a significant difference. In spite of resistance, you never stopped giving your all.

Pastor Susan Lyon. It was truly a blessing, not to mention inspiration, to work with someone completely immersed in the world of homelessness and poverty. Everyone you touched was better off for knowing you. I have fond memories of our sitting on the old couch in the boarding house, working on projects together.

Bob Cote, founder of Step Denver. You showed me the down-and-dirty world of addiction and how to cure it. It was an eye-opening experience I'll never forget. We miss you.

Jessica Backus and Kenzi's Causes. Anytime I needed an inspirational shot in the arm, I came to you and discovered anything is possible.

Drew McCullough and Amanda Muell. I'm indebted to your efforts with FederalSafetyNet.com and teaching me the world of social media.

Paul Kelly. Through boxing and other sports, you helped countless inner-city kids.

The many people and experts I have quoted extensively in the book. You opened up a new world for me, motivating me to be part of a large and diverse team dedicated to wiping out poverty in America. Your research and creative efforts reminded me that we live in a marvelous country where people of diverse backgrounds can work together to improve conditions for the less fortunate among us.

Bob Weinstein. Numbers come easy to me, but I often struggle expressing myself in words. From the outset, you believed in me and my mission so that I could eloquently get my message to all Americans. You went the proverbial extra mile, adopting poverty as your cause so that the book could be pushed over the finish line.

John Long. A brilliant copy editor with extraordinary credentials. I appreciate the hard work you put into my book.

My wife, Richelle. Last but by no means least, I'm eternally grateful for your strength, determination and support. Your quiet but infectious spiritual nature inspired me and everyone else who worked on this project. As a sounding board and motivating force with invaluable input, you helped me make this book an effort I can be proud of. I couldn't have done it without your love and support.

Finally, to all those trying to pull themselves out of poverty and take the next step: Never give up. You can do it, and we want to help.

BIBLIOGRAPHY

Bureau, U.S. Census. 2018. "Income and Poverty in the United States: 2017." U.S. Census Bureau, September.

Eberstadt, Nicholas. 2017. "Our Miserable 21st Century." Commentary, February 15.

FederalSafetyNet.com. n.d. FederalSafetyNet.com. Accessed September 15, 2018. http://federalsafetynet.com/index.html.

Friedman, Milton. 1979. "Free to Choose." Harcourt Books.

Gurteen, Stephen Humphreys. 1882. "A Handbook on Charity Organization." Bibliolife, LLC.

Haskins, Ron. 2012. "Combating Poverty: Understanding New Challenges for Families." Brookings Institution, June 5.

Johnson, Lyndon B. 1964. "Annual Message to the Congress on the State of the Union." January 8.

Kennedy, John F. 1962. Special Message to the Congress on Public Welfare Programs. Washington DC, February 1.

Lupton, Robert D. 2012. "Toxic Charity." New York, NY: HarperCollins Publishers.

Mead, Lawrence. 2001. "From Prophecy to Charity, How to Help the Poor." AEI Press.

Olasky, Marvin. 1992. "The Tragedy of American Compassion." Crossway Books.

Princeton Survey Research Associates International. 2016. "2016 Poverty Survey." American Enterprise Institute and Los Angeles Times, August 18.

Risley, Todd R., and Betty Hart. 1999. "The Social World of Children Learning to Talk." Baltimore, Maryland: Paul H. Brookes Publishing Co., Inc.

Seager, Stephen. 2009. "Street Crazy." Westom Press.

Teresa, Mother. 1997. "No Greater Love." New World Library.

Yankoski, Mike. 2010. "Under the Overpass." Multnomah Books.

Photo Credits

Lyndon Johnson signing the Food Stamp Act of 1964 made available through the Dept. of Agriculture.

Picture of Mother Teresa taken by Manfredo Ferrari.

NOTES

[1] Gallup, 2013, "Most Americans Practice Charitable Giving," *Volunteerism* (December 13), [Internet]. Retrieved January 28, 2017. Available at: http://www.gallup.com/poll/166250/americans-practice-charitable-giving-volunteerism.aspx?g_source=charity&g_medium=search&g_campaign=tiles

[2] Dr. Martin Luther King Jr. 1963, *Strength to Love,* William Collins Sons & Co Ltd., Glasgow. 10.

[3] Shaleec Thomas, Personal interview by Robert S. Pfeiffer, January 28, 2015.

[4] Debbie Stone, Personal interview by Robert S. Pfeiffer, January 28, 2015.

[5] Franklin D. Roosevelt, 1935, Annual Message to Congress, (January 5).

[6] Jason DeParle, 2004, *American Dream,* Penguin Gp, 113.

[7] (Teresa 1997) 97-98.

[8] (Johnson 1964).

[9] Ronald Reagan, 1988, State of the Union Address, (January 25).

[10] Dr. Seuss, 1961, *The Sneetches and Other Stories,* Random House.

[11] Mollie Orshansky, 1965, "Counting the Poor: Another Look at the Poverty Profile," *Social Security Bulletin* (January).

[12] (Bureau 2018), Appendix B.
[13] Ibid., Table 5.

[14] Ibid., Table B1.

[15] Census.Gov., *Dynamics of Economic Well-Being: Poverty 2009–2012,* [Internet], Retrieved July 31, 2015, http://www.census.gov/hhes/www/poverty/publications/dynamics09_12/index.html

[16] (Kennedy 1962)

[17] Bob Cote, Personal interview by Robert S. Pfeiffer in 2011 at Step Denver headquarters.

[18] Milton Friedman, 1967. *Capitalism and Freedom,* The University Chicago Press, 191.

[19] Dr. Martin Luther King Jr, 1968, *Where Do We Go From Here: Chaos or Community?* Beacon Press. 171.

[20] (FederalSafetyNet.com n.d.) See website page – "Living Wage" for a discussion of a living wage set at two times the poverty threshold.
[21] (Bureau 2018), Table 5.

[22] Definition and calculation of the poverty gap is included in Chapter 13.

[23] (FederalSafetyNet.com n.d.) See Webpage – "Living Wage Page".

[24] A summary of all federal welfare programs is shown in Chapter 13.

[25] (Princeton Survey Research Associates International 2016)

[26] *Giving USA*, 2015. [internet], "Americans Donated an Estimated $358.38 Billion to Charity in 2014; Highest Total in Report's 60-year History," (June 29, 2015), https://givingusa.org/giving-usa-2015-press-release-giving-usa-americans-donated-an-estimated-358-38-billion-to-charity-in-2014-highest-total-in-reports-60-year-history/

[27] (Haskins 2012), http://www.brookings.edu/research/testimony/2012/06/05-poverty-families-haskins

[28] Ibid.

[29] Originally named Step 13.

[30] Bob Cote. Personal interview by Robert S. Pfeiffer in 2011 at Step Denver headquarters.

[31] Arthur C. Brooks, "A Nation of Givers," *The American - The Online Magazine of the American Enterprise Institute,* From the March/April 2008 issue, Retrieved October 26, 2014.

[32] (Yankoski 2010) 165.

[33] (Gurteen 1882) 192.

[34] (Eberstadt 2017).

[35] (Gurteen 1882) 34.

[36] Benjamin Franklin, 1753, Letter to Peter Collinson (May 9).

[37] *Merriam-Webster Dictionary*, [Internet], Retrieved January 2, 2016, Available at: http://www.merriam-webster.com/dictionary/pauperize.

[38] (Gurteen 1882) 9.

[39] Benjamin Franklin, 1766, "On the Price of Corn and Management of the Poor," Available at: http://www.vindicatingthefounders.com/library/management-of-poor.html.

[40] (Lupton 2012) 1.

[41] (Gurteen 1882) 24.

[42] (Kennedy 1962).

[43] (Seager 2009) 204.

[44] The United States Conference of Mayors, 2014, "Hunger and Homelessness Survey – A Status Report on Hunger and Homelessness in America's Cities, A 25-City Survey," (December). https://www2.cortland.edu/dotAsset/655b9350-995e-4aae-acd3-298325093c34.pdf

[45] (Seager 2009) 157–161.

[46] (Gurteen 1882) 28.

[47] (Kennedy 1962).

[48] (Gurteen 1882) 12–13.

[49] Personal discussion by Robert S. Pfeiffer with a director of a nonprofit in Denver Colorado who wishes not to be identified.

[50] (Mead 2001) 63.

[51] Ibid., 67.

[52] *The Poverty & Justice Bible*, 1995, Contemporary English Version, American Bible Society, New York, Foreword.

[53] Ibid., The Core, 7.

[54] (Mead 2001) 62.

[55] (Gurteen 1882) 29–30.

[56] Ibid., 31.

[57] (Eberstadt 2017).

[58] (Princeton Survey Research Associates International 2016), https://www.aei.org/publication/2016-poverty-survey/

[59] Lyndon B. Johnson, 1964, Special Message to the Congress Proposing a Nationwide War on the Sources of Poverty, (March 16).

[60] (Olasky 1992) 80.

[61] (Johnson 1964).

[62] (Kennedy 1962)

[63] James Madison, *Annals of Congress,* House of Representatives, 3rd Congress, 1st Session. 170.

[64] (Friedman 1979) 122.

[65] (FederalSafetyNet.com n.d.) See Safety Net Page, for information on programs and costs.

[66] Ibid., See website page— "Poverty Gap."

[67] Ibid., See website page — "Poverty and Spending Over the Years."

[68] Ibid., See Website page — "Welfare Issues."

[69] (Princeton Survey Research Associates International 2016).

[70] (Friedman 1979) 122.

[71] (FederalSafetyNet.com n.d.) See website page — "Welfare Reform."

[72] (Kennedy 1962)

[73] (FederalSafetyNet.com n.d.)See website page – "Poverty Statistics" for additional information and Census Bureau data references.

[74] Mollie Orshansky, 1963, "Children of the Poor," *SSA Bulletin,* July.

[75] (Teresa 1997) 96–97.

[76] Ibid., 97–98.

[77] Ibid., 101.

[78] (Olasky 1992) 197.

[79] *Merriam-Webster Dictionary,* [Internet], Retrieved August 28, 2015. Available here, http://www.merriam-webster.com/dictionary/compassion

[80] (Gurteen 1882) 176.

[81] Ibid., 119.

[82] Ibid., 176.

[83] Ibid., 129.

[84] (Lupton 2012) 128.

[85] Ibid., 63.

[86] (Risley and Hart 1999) 1.

[87] Ibid., 7.

[88] Ibid., 181.

[89] Ibid., 182.

[90] Ibid., 176.

[91] Ibid., 3.

[92] Ibid., 169.

[93] (Olasky 1992) 8.

[94] (Lupton 2012) 191.